AMERICAN
WAR LIBRARY

★ The Iraq War ★

THE
HOME FRONT

Titles in the American War Library series include:

The Iraq War
Life of an American Soldier in Iraq
Rebuilding Iraq
Weapons of War

The American Revolution

The Civil War

The Cold War

The Korean War

The Persian Gulf War

The Vietnam War

The War on Terrorism

World War I

World War II

AMERICAN
WAR LIBRARY

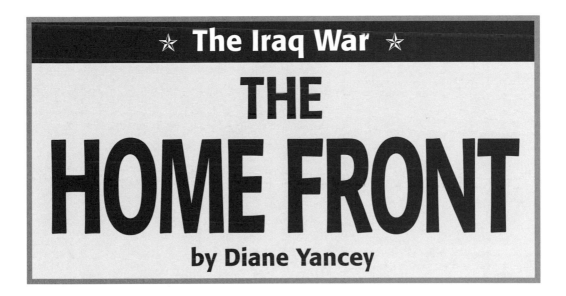

★ The Iraq War ★

THE HOME FRONT

by Diane Yancey

LUCENT BOOKS

An imprint of Thomson Gale, a part of The Thomson Corporation

THOMSON

★

™

GALE

Detroit • New York • San Francisco • San Diego • New Haven, Conn. • Waterville, Maine • London • Munich

For more information, contact
Lucent Books
27500 Drake Rd.
Farmington Hills, MI 48331-3535
Or you can visit our Internet site at http://www.gale.com

LIBRARY OF CONGRESS CATALOGING-IN-PUBLICATION DATA

Yancey, Diane.
  The home front / by Diane Yancey.
    p. cm. — (American war library. Iraq War)
  Includes bibliographical references and index.
Contents: The case for war—"We're all targets"—The war and the media—Heroes at home—The war economy—Division and dissension—A cloudy future.
  ISBN 1-59018-542-0 (hardcover : alk. paper)
  1. Iraq War, 2003—Juvenile literature. I. Title. II. Series.
DS79.763.Y36 2004
956.7044'3373—dc22

36242060414154

2004012503

Printed in the United States of America

⭐ **Contents** ⭐

Foreword 7

Introduction: War from a Homeland Perspective 9

Chapter 1: The Case for War 15

Chapter 2: "We're All Targets" 28

Chapter 3: The War and the Media 40

Chapter 4: Heroes at Home 54

Chapter 5: The War Economy 68

Chapter 6. Division and Dissension 81

Epilogue: A Cloudy Future 95

Notes 100

For Further Reading 110

Works Consulted 111

Index 120

Picture Credits 127

About the Author 128

A Nation Forged by War

The United States, like many nations, was forged and defined by war. Despite Benjamin Franklin's opinion that "There never was a good war or a bad peace," the United States owes its very existence to the War of Independence, one to which Franklin wholeheartedly subscribed. The country forged by war in 1776 was tempered and made stronger by the Civil War in the 1860s.

The Texas Revolution, the Mexican-American War, and the Spanish-American War expanded the country's borders and gave it overseas possessions. These wars made the United States a world power, but this status came with a price, as the nation became a key but reluctant player in both World War I and World War II.

Each successive war further defined the country's role on the world stage. Following World War II, U.S. foreign policy redefined itself to focus on the role of defender, not only of the freedom of its own citizens, but also of the freedom of people everywhere. During the Cold War that followed World War II until the collapse of the Soviet Union, defending the world meant fighting communism. This goal, manifested in the Korean and Vietnam conflicts, proved elusive, and soured the American public on its achievability. As the United States emerged as the world's sole superpower, American foreign policy has been guided less by national interest and more by protecting international human rights. But as involvement in Somalia and Kosovo prove, this goal has been equally elusive.

As a result, the country's view of itself changed. Bolstered by victories in World Wars I and II, Americans first relished the role of protector. But, as war followed war in a seemingly endless procession, Americans began to doubt their leaders, their motives, and themselves. The Vietnam War especially caused people to question the validity of sending its young people to die in places where they were not particularly wanted and for people who did not seem especially grateful.

While the most obvious changes brought about by America's wars have been geopolitical in nature, many other aspects of society have been touched. War often does not bring about change directly, but acts instead like the catalyst in a chemical reaction, accelerating changes already in progress.

Some of these changes have been societal. The role of women in the United States had been slowly changing, but World War II put thousands into the workforce and into uniform. They might have gone back to being housewives after the war, but equality, once experienced, would not be forgotten.

Likewise, wars have accelerated technological change. The necessity for faster airplanes and more destructive bombs led to the development of jet planes and nuclear energy. Artificial fibers developed for parachutes in the 1940s were used in clothing of the 1950s.

Lucent Books' American War Library covers key wars in the development of the nation. Each war is covered in several volumes, to allow for more detail, context, and to provide volumes on often neglected subjects, such as the kamikazes of World War II, or the weapons used in the Civil War. As with all Lucent books, notes, annotated bibliographies, and appendixes such as glossaries give students a launching point for further research. In addition, sidebars and archival photographs enhance the text. Together, each volume in The American War Library will aid students in understanding how America's wars have shaped and changed its politics, economics, and society.

★ Introduction ★

War from a Homeland Perspective

O n Sunday, December 14, 2003, Americans awoke to the news that Iraqi dictator Saddam Hussein, in hiding since the fall of his repressive regime nine months earlier, had been captured by U.S. soldiers in Iraq. All those who turned on their television sets saw pictures of the once-defiant dictator being examined by military doctors, his mouth probed with a tongue depressor, his shaggy hair checked for lice.

Shocked by his defeated appearance, people from coast to coast nevertheless rejoiced over his seizure. A sign that popped up on the front of a dry cleaning establishment in a small town in Washington State expressed the nation's mood. "God Bless America. We Got Him," it read. "I have been waiting for this for the last 35 years," [1] said Alan Zangana, an Iraqi who fled his country to live in the United States in 1981, two years after Saddam came to power.

Triumph or Miscalculation?

The day Saddam was captured was a triumphant one in a war that Americans watched with conflicted feelings from the very beginning. In the fall of 2002, Congress had authorized President George W. Bush to use military might to disarm Saddam, and troops began to be deployed to the Middle East. In threatening war, Bush hoped to force the dictator to comply with United Nations (UN) resolutions that demanded Saddam turn over any weapons of mass destruction (WMDs)—chemical, biological, and nuclear weapons—that he possessed.

Bush's threat failed, but so did efforts to gain support for war from the United Nations and other world powers. They disagreed that Saddam posed an imminent (immediate) threat to the world. Determinedly, Bush went ahead with a plan to disarm Saddam without UN support, leaving many Americans to wonder if he was doing the right thing. "I hope they made the right decision in what we are doing because in doing this, we're losing a lot of ties with other countries," said Meagan MacLeod of Massachusetts. "I don't want a World War III." [2]

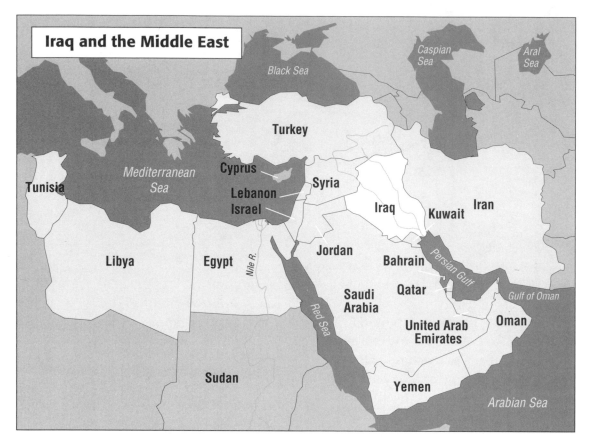

Iraq and the Middle East

U.S. military leaders seemed confident that the president had made the right decision, and they indicated that pulling off a successful campaign against Saddam was well within their powers. Innocent Iraqis would not be targeted. The initial bombardment, designed to inspire "shock and awe" due to its scope and power, could be focused on specific government and military sites. The war would be carried out by America's best—thousands of highly trained young men and women who were equipped with the most up-to-date equipment in the world.

When the opening salvos began in March 2003, the scene was indeed impressive. Warplanes and ships launched hundreds of cruise missiles that rained down on Baghdad, knocking out water supplies, electricity, communication services, roads, bridges, and other essentials. "The night sky . . . pulsed with crimson fireballs and Iraqi tracer fire," read a *Newsweek* article written by reporter Melinda Liu. "An entire riverbank of government buildings . . . disintegrated as I watched from an upper floor [of my hotel]."[3]

By May 1, American hopes for a short war soared as ground troops captured major cities and drove Saddam and his Baath Party supporters from power. The news ran pictures of young American soldiers in tanks rolling through Baghdad and picking their way through the glittering palaces that had been the dictator's homes. "It's great actually, to know we are in [Saddam's] house and he doesn't want us to be here,"[4] said Private Daniel Dunn.

With the fall of Baghdad, Bush and U.S. military leaders declared that the major fighting was over. Even though Saddam had escaped, the campaign had been victorious, they said. The U.S. soldiers had accomplished their mission. Iraq would soon be a beacon of peace and democracy to other turbulent Middle Eastern countries.

The coming weeks and months proved them wrong, however. Terrorists rushed into the country, and Iraqis began agitating for the Americans to leave. Bombings, ambushes, and other kinds of guerrilla warfare became the order of the day. Saddam's capture in December was only a brief high point in an otherwise discouraging month. As American troops struggled to keep order, the numbers

A group of Iraqis stands in front of a Baghdad building destroyed during a U.S. air strike in March 2003.

of dead and wounded continued to grow. "It's hard to see headway," said Sky Schermerhorn of the Second Battalion, stationed in Baghdad. "I'd like to see these people enjoy what I have on a daily basis. But I don't know that anything we've accomplished since we've been here was worth [risking my life for]."[5]

A Different Perspective

On the home front, Americans experienced the war from a very different perspective than did the troops in Iraq. Some found the U.S. military's performance thrilling and inspirational. "I am so proud of our brave service men and women who were willing to follow their Commander-in-Chief and fight to liberate the Iraqi people from Saddam Hussein and his reign of terror," said Assemblyman Dennis Mountjoy of California.[6]

Others struggled with different emotions. "This is a nightmare, it's just a nightmare," said Michael Lopercio, whose son was in the army. "He's got two years left in the service and I'm visualizing that he may spend two years in the most dangerous place on Earth."[7]

The media played a central role in shaping public awareness of the war, bringing the most dramatic elements of the conflict into everyone's living room every day. The media were also a distraction, reminding Americans that there were other issues to be dealt with besides war. Reports on homeland security let citizens know they were still vulnerable to terrorist attacks. News of the unsteady economy and the growing budget deficit made them wish their leaders were free to concentrate on domestic rather than foreign issues. "Let's get it [the war] over with and let's get back to the economy,"[8] said Judy Diamonde of New York.

The war's progress was on everyone's mind as the presidential election of 2004

Differing Viewpoints

The capture of Saddam Hussein marked a high point in the war in Iraq, but it did not make the conflict less controversial. The following two letters to the editor were published under the heading "A Tyrant Captured" in *Newsweek* magazine a few weeks after the event.

"Can we all agree that Iraq's meanest, cruelest and deadliest weapon of mass destruction was found in a hole on December 13? Congratulations go to America's bravest men and women for yet another job well done, and to our commander in chief who has the courage of his convictions." Robert Kuesel, Milwaukee, Wisconsin.

"Saddam Hussein's capture has not been cheap. Hundreds of young Americans have lost their lives and thousands have been seriously maimed. Thousands of Iraqis have been killed and more than $100 billion has been spent on the war and reconstruction. Meanwhile, the weapons of mass destruction have not been found, world-wide terrorist activity has not decreased and Osama bin Laden has not been caught. As the cost in lives and money continues to mount, several questions must be asked: Was the capture of Saddam worth the price? Are we safer? Are the Iraqis safer?" Dick Meis, Murrieta, California.

loomed on the horizon. Americans were challenged to decide whether or not they wanted the lives of their soldiers in the hands of the current administration. Changing leadership while involved in a war abroad seemed risky. On the other hand, some wondered whether there was someone wiser and more responsible than Bush to guide them through such a difficult time.

The questions produced ever-increasing debate as time passed. The war was immoral.

U.S. soldiers assess the damage outside a police station near Baghdad after a car-bomb attack in November 2003.

The war was doing a great deal of good. U.S. involvement should end. The nation needed to stay the course, however long it might take. Through all the debate, however, there was still some common ground. One commentator noted, "Both sides in the U.S. presidential election need to make clear to

Paying Dearly

As Americans debated whether a war with Iraq was necessary or not, correspondent Fouad Ajami postulated that the war was inevitable, given past U.S. policies. Ajami explores the war's roots in "A Chronicle of a War Foretold" in *U.S. News & World Report*.

In retrospect, it is hard to know when this inevitable war against the regime of Saddam Hussein really began. Perhaps the beginning might have come back in 1991, when American military power spared the Iraqi ruler and left him to the idle hope of a "palace coup" and to the judgment of his brutalized people. America had called on Iraqis to take matters into their hands; they did so, only to be betrayed and drowned in blood and terror. In the north and south, the Kurds and the Shiites risked life and limb; the American response was one of utter indifference. Of these two rebellions, General Colin Powell, then chairman of the Joint Chiefs of Staff, would later write: "Neither revolt had a chance. Nor, frankly, was their success a goal of our policy." We now pay dearly for that indifference and abdication.

America's enemies, to former and present allies, and to the American people as well, one simple thing: No matter who wins the election, terrorists [must] lose. There can be disagreements galore, but no real divisions in the war on terror."[9]

Americans shared another common cause, as well. Concern for the troops was an obligation that no one shirked and no one questioned. Bringing them back to safety was a universal goal, and all wanted to accomplish that goal as quickly as possible. Journalist Nancy Gibbs observed, "In a year when it felt at times as if we had nothing in common anymore, we were united in this hope; that our men and women at arms might soon come safely home, because their job was done."[10]

☆ Chapter 1 ☆

The Case for War

After terrorists struck the World Trade Center and the Pentagon on September 11, 2001, killing and injuring thousands of people and doing billions of dollars in damage, most Americans were united in the decision to go to war. Saudi Arabian radical Osama bin Laden and his terrorist organization, al Qaeda, had carried out a heinous attack on U.S. soil. The Taliban, the fundamentalist Muslim regime in Afghanistan, where bin Laden took refuge, defiantly refused to cooperate in the capture of the Saudi terrorist. "Public opinion remains firmly behind the White House: Polls taken during the first twelve hours of the attacks showed nearly 90 percent of Americans support the retaliatory strikes against Osama bin Laden and the Taliban,"[11] reported *Time* magazine on October 10, 2001.

Such was not the case as the nation prepared for war in Iraq in 2003. Everyone from world leaders to ordinary Americans questioned whether the war was a choice or a necessity. Did Saddam pose a danger that had

to be immediately confronted, they asked, or could other options be carefully considered before taking extreme action. Richard Haas, former director of policy planning for the State Department, supported the latter view. "At its core it was a war of choice," he said in November 2003. "We did not have to go to war against Iraq, certainly not when we did. There were other options: to rely on other policy tools, to delay attacking, or both."[12]

Secretary of Defense Donald Rumsfeld disagreed. "The Iraqi regime is a grave and gathering danger," he said early in 2003. "With each passing day, Saddam Hussein advances his arsenal of weapons of mass destruction, and could pass them along to terrorists. If he is allowed to do so, the result could be the deaths not of 3,000 people, as on September 11th, but 30,000 or 300,000 or more innocent people."[13]

War Against Terror

President George W. Bush was one of those who sided with Rumsfeld. Even before the war in Afghanistan began, he thought the war on terror might extend to Iraq before all was said and done. As early as September 15, 2001, he warned Americans that the fight to root out terrorism would not be short or easy. On October 9, 2001, the president expressed his point of view through U.S. ambassador to the United Nations John Negroponte, who wrote in a letter to the UN Security Council, "We may find that our self-defense requires further actions with respect to other organizations and other states."[14]

Negroponte's remarks were not widely reported, and Americans did not pay much attention to the possibilities they raised. They were listening, however, when, in his State of the Union address in January 2002, Bush spoke of regimes that sponsored terror. He named North Korea, Iran, and Iraq as an "axis of evil," and expanded on the problems

In his 2002 State of the Union address, President Bush identified Iraq as part of a coalition he called the "axis of evil."

they could cause in the future. He stated, "By seeking weapons of mass destruction, these regimes pose a grave and growing danger. They could provide these arms to terrorists, giving them the means to match their hatred. They could attack our allies or attempt to blackmail the United States. In any of these cases, the price of indifference would be catastrophic."[15]

Despite the president's reference, Americans pushed the thought of Iraq as an enemy aside. They were caught up in the war in Afghanistan, where special forces and conventional soldiers were fighting to topple the Taliban and capture bin Laden.

The fight was fierce and considered successful by most. In the course of three months, a UN force had pushed the Taliban out of power and Osama bin Laden and his operatives into hiding. At the end of a year, military action had settled into sporadic attacks on pockets of guerrilla fighters. UN troops remained in the country, ensuring that the newly formed transition government was safe and able to lead. They also continued the search for Bin Laden and Taliban head Mohammed Omar.

A Wider Effort

As the crisis passed in Afghanistan, the focus shifted to terrorism in other parts of the world. In October 2002, Americans were shocked when an al Qaeda–sponsored car bombing in Bali, Indonesia, claimed almost two hundred lives and revealed that country to be a hideout for Islamic radicals. The bombing of a Tunisian synagogue in April 2002 was traced to al Qaeda as well. In response to those attacks and those of September 11, intelligence and law enforcement operatives tracked down and captured or killed al Qaeda operatives in countries ranging from Pakistan and the Sudan to Germany, Belgium, and Spain.

As he went after terrorists, Bush did not ignore his "axis of evil" nations. Iran did not demand immediate attention because it had increased its cooperation with the West since the election of reformist president Mohammed Khatami in 1997. In October 2002, however, U.S. officials confronted the North Korean government with evidence showing that it had been secretly pursuing a nuclear weapons development program in violation of a 1994 agreement. Hostilities between the two countries heated up, but diplomacy eased the tension as China and South Korea took the lead in mediating a solution to the problem.

Thus, Iraq was Bush's main focus in 2002. The president asserted that Saddam Hussein was an unstable leader who possessed weapons of mass destruction. Early that year, he began demanding that Saddam allow UN weapons inspectors back into Iraq to continue their search for the weapons the dictator allegedly possessed. Inspectors had originally entered the country in 1991, but Saddam had repeatedly blocked their efforts since then. Samuel R. Berger, assistant to President Bill Clinton, stated, "Baghdad has engaged the . . . inspectors in a high stakes game of cat-and-mouse—lying to them, harassing them, delaying their access

In December 2002 UN inspectors search for evidence of weapons of mass destruction in Iraq.

to sites, flagrantly destroying evidence."[16] In 1998 Saddam called a halt to inspections. In ensuing years, he continued to ignore UN resolutions that called for him to disarm, and even shot at U.S. planes policing the no-fly zones over Iraq.

On September 12, 2002, Bush issued an ultimatum. He stated that unless the dictator complied completely with UN demands, "action would be unavoidable." "The purposes of the United States should not be doubted," he said. "The Security Council resolutions will be enforced—the just demands of peace and security will be met."[17] Faced with such pressure, Saddam allowed the inspectors back into Iraq. Almost im-

mediately, however, he began throwing up new roadblocks to their progress.

Preemptive War

Bush's tough stance toward Iraq took many Americans by surprise. They were impressed by his firmness, but did not know what to think about the new defense doctrine—preemptive war—he introduced in 2002. By its standards, the United States could strike first against another country in order to prevent a terrorist act. "Facing clear evidence of peril, we cannot wait for the final proof, the smoking gun that could come in the form of a mushroom cloud [atomic bomb]," he said.[18]

Some people, such as Senator Edward Kennedy of Massachusetts, categorically opposed preemptive war on moral grounds. Kennedy believed that preemptive war was just another name for aggression. "Might does not make right," he said. "America cannot write its own rules for the modern world. . . . It would give other nations, from Russia, to India, to Pakistan an excuse to violate fundamental principles of civilized international behavior."[19]

Other Americans were uncomfortable being in the same category as nations who had made the first move in attacking or invading others in the past. Nazi Germany, Japan, and the Communist Soviet Union, for instance, had been considered aggressors who had to be defeated or blocked. The United States had always prided itself on being a protector. It went to war only to help a weaker ally or after it had been attacked or seriously threatened.

Preemptive war seemed to set a dangerous standard whereby all kinds of behavior could be rationalized in the name of fighting terrorism. Nevertheless, most Americans felt that exceptions sometimes had to be made for special circumstances. They also noted that at least one respected

Doctrine of Preemption

George W. Bush's push for preemptive war in Iraq raised many questions. Columnist David M. Shribman explores two of them in an article entitled "Bush Doctrine Slipping Under Political Radar" published in the *Boston Globe*.

The Bush Doctrine is not only a great departure from American tradition. It also raises important questions that Congress and the public have not yet debated. Among them:

Who gets to take preemptive action? The United States asserts the right to do so. But in international practice, nations that claim a right for themselves are assumed to be willing to grant that right to other nations. The Bush Doctrine is silent on this subject. But the more the United States asserts this right, the more others are going to believe that it is their right as well. The United States would be immensely uneasy, for example, if India or Pakistan asserted that right against the other. And in the new age, when America's foes are more likely to be groups like al-Qaida than nations like Russia, the Bush Doctrine might inadvertently be providing the nation's most bitter rival with what it believes is a moral justification for terrorist activities that Americans will surely regard as immoral.

Does might make right? At the heart of the Bush Doctrine is the notion that the United States can take preemptive action because it has the power to do so. The United States has no rivals to its military power anywhere in the world today. But American power around the globe isn't based on military might alone. It is built, too, on the power of American ideas, the power of America's freedom and the power of American culture. The nation still must debate whether the power of American values could be undermined around the world if it asserts that the power to act unilaterally [alone] is the same as the right to act unilaterally.

president in the past had believed that pre-emption was sometimes justified. President John F. Kennedy had been ready to issue a preemptive strike against the Soviet Union during the Cuban Missile Crisis in 1962. He said: "Neither the United States of America nor the world community of nations can tolerate deliberate deception and offensive threats on the part of any nation, large or small. We no longer live in a world where only the actual firing of weapons represents a sufficient challenge to a nation's security."[20]

Give Us More Facts

Despite reservations about preemptive war, there seemed to be little doubt at the time that Saddam Hussein had weapons of mass destruction and was hiding them. General Wesley Clark stated in January 2003, "There's a lot of stuff hidden in a lot of different places. . . . People in Iraq [know where it is]. The scientists know some of it. Some of the military, . . . some of Saddam Hussein's security organizations. There's a big organization in place to cover and deceive and prevent anyone from knowing about this."[21]

Past events had proved that Saddam was a threat to his neighbors. In the Iran-Iraq War of 1980–1988, for instance, he had repeatedly used mustard gas, cyanide, and deadly nerve agents such as sarin against the Iranian army. During one of the battles, an estimated five thousand residents of Halabja, a Kurdish town in northern Iraq, died and another ten thousand were injured as a result of a chemical assault.

According to intelligence reports (information from undercover agents, spy planes, and other sources), Saddam was also working to obtain nuclear weapons in 2002. With those, he could inflict catastrophic harm on the world. U.S. experts pointed to aluminum tubes he had recently acquired, insisting that they could be made to serve as rotors in centrifuges used to enrich uranium. Saddam's government insisted that the tubes were destined to be used as rocket bodies for multiple rocket launchers, which are conventional weapons, but many Americans assumed they were lying. One observer noted, "The answer to Hussein is a simple one. He, and all like him, must not be allowed to hold the world hostage. He must be stopped as must all terrorism."[22]

After considering the threats, most Americans decided they could accept a case for preemptive war, as long as Saddam was on the verge of attack. Bush had not made a convincing case for such a possibility, however. He had not presented the nation with documents, pictures, taped conversations, or anything else that proved plans for an attack were imminent.

Some did not believe such proof existed. They believed that Saddam posed no immediate threat to the world. Rather, they thought the president wanted to "take care of old business" while he was in office. His father, President George H.W. Bush, had long been criticized for not definitively defeating Saddam in the Persian Gulf War of 1991. Perhaps his son wanted to remedy that for his father's sake. Columnist Ciro Scotti

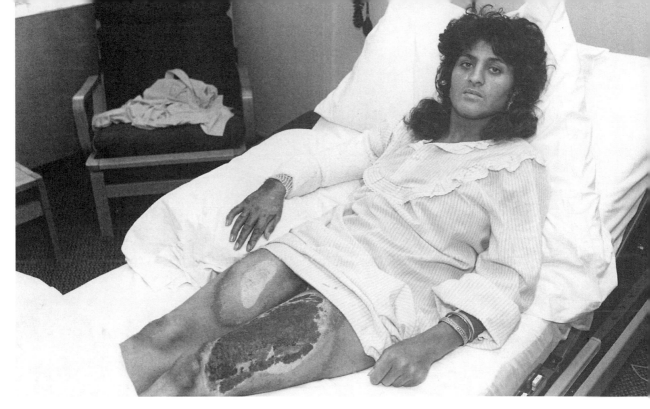

A Kurdish woman displays the wounds she sustained during Saddam's 1988 chemical assault on the town of Halabja.

wrote, "Saddam isn't just an America-hating, chemical-weapons-building, vicious dictator, and sponsor of all manner of global terror. He's the man who put a bunch of doubts into folks' heads about the validity of the Persian Gulf war triumph. Saddam was behind a failed assassination attempt on Bush's father in 1993, U.S. intelligence agencies say. Saddam is a bad man."[23]

Other Americans were willing to give the president the benefit of the doubt. If he had information about an imminent attack by Saddam, they reasoned, that information was likely classified. To reveal it to the public might also give Saddam information that could be used against the nation. "He is keeping a lot from us to protect us,"[24] said Richard Dietz of Michigan. Nevertheless, most wanted to have as much information as possible before committing to something as serious as war. Paul Dellevigne of Pennsylvania observed:

The idea of removing a dictator who is only known for destruction and death is a good idea. But our President must understand how important it is to make it clear to America and the United Nations what the exact threat is. Making vague statements will not justify a unilateral attack, and it will not convince the United Nations that an attack is justified. And everyone must recognize that an unjustified attack against a sovereign nation may inspire even more attacks against our homeland.[25]

There were those Americans, too, who felt that debating questions of imminent threat was beside the point. Saddam might not be planning to attack immediately, but he was still a brutal dictator. In their view, allowing him to continue to rule and live in luxury while his people suffered under his tyranny was unthinkable. Those who opposed going to war with him were helping to maintain an intolerable injustice. Removing him was a responsibility the United States should have shouldered long ago. "War is an awful thing," wrote journalist Andrew Sullivan. "But it isn't the most awful thing." [26]

No Clear and Present Danger

By March 2003, polls in the United States showed that 75 percent of all Americans supported the president's push for a preemptive war. Their support, however, remained subject to obtaining UN backing for the campaign. Getting that support could take time, but a few extra weeks seemed acceptable, since it seemed unlikely that Saddam would strike immediately. On the other hand, a united front—and the threat of military action from the whole world—might pressure him to disarm. He might even be persuaded to step down.

If pressure failed, UN backing would legitimatize the war and would also provide additional troops to help in the fighting and rebuilding that would follow. "The costs in all areas will be much greater, as will the political risks, both domestic and international, if we end up going it alone or with

Many Americans regarded Saddam Hussein as a brutal dictator who had to be removed from power.

only one or two countries," [27] former secretary of state James Baker stated in 2002.

Gaining UN support was easier said than done, however. UN inspectors did not advocate an immediate war. They said that, given more time, they were hopeful that they would make progress in disarming Saddam. Influential member countries such as France, Germany, and Russia particularly opposed taking part in any military action. Germany, with its history of aggression in World War II, emphatically rejected any preemptive undertakings. All three countries regarded small concessions by Iraq—such as destroying several banned al-Samoud missiles—as signs that inspections, negotiation, and continuing pressure to disarm were working. "In its current situation, does Iraq—controlled and inspected as it is—pose a clear and present danger to the region? I don't believe so," [28] said French president Jacques Chirac.

France, Germany, and Russia were not the only nations that refused to follow the United States into war with Iraq. Canada, Belgium, and Norway, all longtime allies of the United States, were also opposed. Despite such opposition, however, a large number of countries did indicate their support, forming a "coalition of the willing" that included Britain, Japan, Australia, Spain, and forty-one other nations. Prime Minister John Howard of Australia expressed his point of view on the day the bombing began: "I passionately believe that action must be taken to disarm Iraq. Not only will it take dangerous weapons from that country, but it will send a clear signal to other rogue states and terrorist groups, like Al Qaeda, which clearly want such weapons, that the world is prepared to take a stand." [29] Contributions from the coalition included troops, logistical support, and promises to assist with reconstruction efforts.

"Good-bye France"

For Americans who supported going to war, the United Nations' position seemed un-reasonable. France, whose leaders and citizens were particularly outspoken against the United States, was the focus of much criticism. Some Americans cited evidence that France had economic ties to Iraq, and thus was afraid of losing money and a valuable client if Saddam were overthrown. Some attributed the country's position to anti-American sentiment that dated back

Antiwar activists in Paris, France, wave a tattered and graffiti-covered American flag to express their opposition to war in Iraq.

many decades. That sentiment was based on France's distrust of America's power and policies which sometimes conflicted with French views on world affairs. "It is French policy to diminish our influence in Europe and in the world, and to shape the European Union as a counterweight to the United States,"[30] said Pentagon policy adviser Richard Perle.

Anti-French feeling sparked all kinds of reactions in the United States. The word "French" was removed from some restaurant menus. French fries were renamed "Freedom fries," and French toast became "Liberty toast." One restaurant owner poured French wine into the street. One French native had anti-French graffiti scrawled on her garage door.

Some American families refused to host visits by French exchange students. Other people, like one woman who posted the following message on the Internet, wrote letters and editorials to express their outrage.

> To hell with French wine and Perrier [water], (both of which I PREVIOUSLY purchased) and also to French fashions and perfume. I adore French perfume but have asked my dear husband not to buy any more French fragrances. I will have to find something else. I also will not serve any more French cheese at parties. I have always felt the French were a bit arrogant and unfriendly, but still admired the art and flair of the country. Not anymore. . . . Good-bye France. I disown you.[31]

Even the Pentagon scaled back its presence at the 2003 Paris Air Show, the global defense industry's largest and oldest networking event for aerospace and defense in-

Freedom Fries and Liberty Dressing

America's rejection of all things French during the war in Iraq was not the first such reaction in time of war. Author Hugh Rawson details other instances of patriotism expressed through language and food in his article "The Road to Freedom Fries," published in *American Heritage* magazine.

> Freedom fries and liberty dressing continue a well-established culinary tradition. During World War I, patriotic Americans took to eating liberty cabbage instead of sauerkraut and liberty sandwiches instead of hamburgers. . . . Naturally, frankfurters and wieners were sold more often as hot dogs during this period.
>
> The very word German became, so to speak, verboten [forbidden]. Thus, German toast was dropped as an alternative name for French toast, German shepherds began to be called Alsatians, though such dogs are not native to Alsace, and children started coming down with liberty measles instead of that other kind.
>
> There was less of this semantic tomfoolery during World War II. True, the collaborationist [pro-German] government in [Vichy] France gave Vichy such a bad name that the 1941 edition of *The Escoffier Cook Book* opted for Créme Gauloise instead of vichyssoise [a cold soup], but Eisenhower herring never displaced Bismarck herring, and the National Association of Meat Merchants declined to adopt a proposal to change hamburger to defense steak.

dustries. Officials also hinted that France's lack of support could lead to trade sanctions, including higher tariffs and quotas.

U.S. secretary of state Colin Powell tries to persuade the UN to support a war against Iraq. His efforts failed.

"We Must Not Fail"

The Bush administration made its most significant effort to gain both U.S. and UN approval for war on February 5, 2003. On that day, Secretary of State Colin Powell presented to the UN Security Council what he claimed was indisputable proof that Saddam posed a grave and immediate threat to world peace.

Powell showed pictures of alleged mobile weapons laboratories and weapons bunkers that reportedly contained chemical and biological materials. He also offered intelligence that tied Saddam to terrorism. Saddam had paid thousands of dollars to families of Palestinian terrorists killed while fighting against Israel. In the 1990s Saddam's agents also allegedly met repeatedly with highly placed al Qaeda operatives to discuss issues such as terrorist training and the use of chemical weapons. Al Qaeda operatives were identified working with Ansar al-Islam, a militant Islamic extremist group in northern Iraq.

Powell went on to point out that Saddam had not complied with UN Resolution 1441, which required him to allow UN inspectors total access to the country while also providing them with complete details of Iraqi weapons of mass destruction, delivery systems, and programs. Taking that into account, a UN response was long overdue. The secretary of state ended his address with these words: "We must not shrink from whatever is ahead of us. We must not fail in our duty and our responsibility to the citizens of the countries that are represented by this body."[32]

Despite his eloquence, Powell did not sway his audience. France, Germany, and Russia continued to believe that negotiation was better than force. "The use of force can only be a final recourse," insisted French foreign minister Dominique de Villepin. Germany's foreign minister, Joschka Fischer, emphasized, "We need a tough regime of intensive inspections that can guarantee the full and lasting disarmament of Iraq's weapons of mass destruction. By tightening inspections, we are creating an opportunity for a peaceful solution."[33]

Countdown to War

Despite the widespread opposition, Powell's speech triggered America's countdown to war. U.S. troops had been preparing for combat in the Persian Gulf region since December 2002. On January 28, 2003, in his State of the Union address, Bush announced that the United States was ready to attack

To Deceive, Not Disarm

In remarks made to the UN Security Council on February 5, 2003, Secretary of State Colin Powell presented what he believed were compelling reasons for immediate war in Iraq. Powell's entire presentation, entitled "Remarks to the United Nations Security Council," can be found on the U.S. Department of State Web site. An excerpt follows:

> Resolution 1441 gave Iraq one last chance, one last chance to come into compliance or to face serious consequences. . . . This Council placed the burden on Iraq to comply and disarm, and not on the inspectors to find that which Iraq has gone out of its way to conceal for so long. Inspectors are inspectors; they are not detectives. . . .
>
> We know that Saddam Hussein has what is called "a Higher Committee for Monitoring the Inspection Teams." Think about that. Iraq has a high-level committee to monitor the inspectors who were sent in to monitor Iraq's disarmament—not to cooperate with them, not to assist them, but to spy on them and keep them from doing their jobs.
>
> The committee reports directly to Saddam Hussein. It . . . includes Lieutenant General Amir al-Sa'di, an advisor to Saddam. . . . It was General Sa'di who last fall publicly pledged that Iraq was prepared to cooperate unconditionally with inspectors. Quite the contrary, Sa'di's job is not to cooperate; it is to deceive, not to disarm, but to undermine the inspectors; not to support them, but to frustrate them and to make sure they learn nothing.

Iraq even without a UN mandate. On February 24—nineteen days after Powell's UN speech—Bush, British prime minister Tony Blair, and Spanish prime minister José Maria Aznar submitted a proposed resolution to the UN Security Council stating that "Iraq has failed to take the final opportunity afforded to it in Resolution 1441,"[34] and that it was now time to authorize use of military force against Saddam.

On March 17 all diplomatic efforts ceased when Bush delivered another ultimatum to Saddam Hussein—leave Iraq within forty-eight hours or face an attack. The president promised Americans, "The tyrant will soon be gone. . . . The terrorist threat to America and the world will be diminished the moment that Saddam Hussein is disarmed."[35]

Americans could only hope he was right. War seemed inevitable, but many feared that a war to remove Saddam would not necessarily make the United States a safer place. Sending troops into Iraq could increase Muslim hostility toward the West. Many people in the Middle East already believed the war on terror was a war against Islam. Many also remembered and resented the U.S. presence in the Middle East during the Persian Gulf War. Another war could precipitate more terrorist attacks in America. "There is a lot of animosity out there toward the United States," said a senior law enforcement official in Washington, D.C. "These groups and individuals want to attack us anyway, and this could give them the perfect excuse."[36]

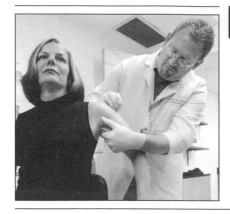

Chapter 2

"We're All Targets"

The bombs and missiles that rained down on Baghdad on March 20, 2003, put an end to discussions about whether or not the United States should take military action against Iraq. The campaign was a fact of life. The nation was involved in another war.

With this realization came a heightened sense of fear. September 11 had proven that the United States was not beyond the reach of a terrorist strike. Intelligence sources indicated that Saddam Hussein had weapons of mass destruction. The Bush administration insisted he was an imminent threat. If so, he might strike out at the United States in a last desperate attempt to save himself and his regime. Americans could only hope that new national security measures that had been put in place would be enough to protect them from such an attack. William Taylor, a retired U.S. Army colonel and military analyst at the Center for Strategic and International Studies, predicted, "Saddam wouldn't go down without using his ace in

the hole, which is a Scud missile with chemical or biological weapons on it."[37]

Saddam—or Someone Else

Americans worried about what Saddam might do if he attacked the United States. The dictator did not have missiles that would reach across the Atlantic, but he had other weapons that could be just as devastating. Experts postulated that one of his agents could easily slip across the U.S. border from Canada or Mexico and contaminate American food or water with something deadly, such as botulinum bacteria, that would produce a large number of deaths. There was also the possibility that Iraqi agents could bring small vials of the smallpox virus (which Saddam allegedly possessed) into the country and start an epidemic. Journalists Daniel Klaidman and Christopher Dickey suggested a scenario, "A small team of Iraqi operatives could be injected with smallpox and sent to America," they postulated. "All they'd have to do is hang out in crowds and slowly die [infecting others as they did so]."[38]

Some experts laughed at the notion of Iraqi agents striking the homeland. They claimed that such agents had been rather inept in the past when it came to carrying out undercover activities. For example, when Saddam attempted the assassination of former president George H.W. Bush in 1993, he hired killers who were amateurs and who could easily be traced to Iraq's intelligence agency. "The Iraqis are the Marx Brothers of intelligence services,"[39] said Richard Clarke, an antiterrorism expert. No one ruled out the possibility that Saddam could sell chemical or biological weapons to more capable operatives, however. Al Qaeda, for instance, was an organization that had an unparalleled reputation for careful planning and successful attacks. The Bush administration contended that ties existed between Saddam and al Qaeda. Provided with a weapon that Saddam had perfected, one of its operatives could do unimaginable damage.

No one could dispute the fact that al Qaeda terrorists lived in the United States. After Khalid Shaikh Mohammed, al Qaeda's director of global operations, was arrested in March 2003, U.S. authorities learned the scope of the organization's infiltration into their country. Operatives lived in Baltimore, Maryland; Columbus, Ohio; and Peoria, Illinois. They lived and plotted in safe houses such as one found near Buffalo, New York. Family members helped by renting post office boxes, buying cars, and providing other services so plotters could remain undercover.

Some al Qaeda agents had lived in the United States a long time, were familiar with life there, and thus were almost beyond suspicion. For instance, Ali al-Marri of Peoria, Illinois, went to college in the United States and had a wife and children with whom he traveled, giving the impression of being a regular family man. After al-Marri was named by Shaikh Mohammed, the FBI learned that he served as a contact man for new al Qaeda agents arriving in the United States. He had also scoped out reservoirs, dams, and railroads for possible strikes. He was eventually arrested, classed as an enemy combatant, and imprisoned.

Without Fear

After *Time* magazine ran an article entitled "A Nation on Edge," detailing how Americans feared another terrorist attack, Curtis Taylor of Muncie, Indiana, responded with the following letter to the editor, also published in *Time*. He insisted that fear was not a preoccupation for many in the early days of the war in Iraq.

"A Nation on Edge" depicted the U.S. as living in fear. This is not the America I see and hear every day. The people buying duct tape and plastic sheeting are the same ones who waited in line to pay $4 a gallon for gas after 9/11. While Osama bin Laden and Saddam Hussein are cowering in a cave or living in a bunker, the majority of Americans are living their daily lives without fear. On a recent trip, I saw a bumper sticker that sums it up best: AIN'T SKEERD.

Iyman Faris, a naturalized U.S. citizen from Kashmir, was another al Qaeda agent identified by Shaikh Mohammed. Living in the United States, Faris had found work as a truck driver, and had been given the task by al Qaeda of buying acetylene torches to cut suspension cables on bridges. He had also been told to buy tools that could be used to bend railroad tracks. Faris failed to get either, and escaped to Pakistan where he was eventually captured. He was returned to the United States, pleaded guilty, and was sentenced to prison.

Iyman Faris, a naturalized U.S. citizen living in Ohio, was arrested in June 2003 as a suspected al Qaeda operative.

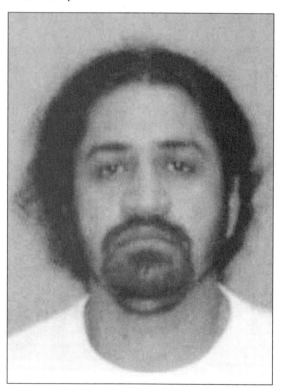

Some potential terrorists were born in the United States. In February 2004 Ryan Anderson, a Washington State native and a U.S. army national guardsman, was arrested for attempted espionage. The government contended that he tried to pass information to al Qaeda. In March 2004 Susan Lindauer of Maryland was arrested after allegedly engaging in transactions with the Iraqi government with the intent of aiding Iraq in the war.

Personal Preparedness

With the possibility of danger everywhere, caution was the watchword for Americans as the war in Iraq began. Many people chose not to travel. Events that could draw large crowds, such as the Washington, D.C., marathon, were cancelled. Because of security concerns, Major League Baseball also changed its plans to fly two teams to Japan to play their season-opening series in spring 2003. Commissioner Bud Selig said, "Given the uncertainty that now exists throughout the world, we believe the safest course of action for the players involved and the many staff personnel who must work the games is to reschedule the opening series."[40]

Responsible for responding to an attack, state and local agencies worked to ensure that their emergency systems were as well developed as possible. Vaccines were stockpiled to be used on the public if a bioterrorist attack occurred. Medical officials and hospital workers carried out disaster response drills. These involved first-response teams—nurses, doctors, paramedics, and the like—who had been trained to recognize symptoms of anthrax, nerve agents, and poisons, and would be first on the scene. By September 2003 all fifty states had bioterrorism preparedness plans, including plans for mass vaccination in the event of attack.

Individuals ensured that they were prepared as well. Many took college, fire department, or Red Cross disaster preparedness classes, where they learned how to put together survival kits, how to wear gas masks, and which rooms of the house were the safest in which to seek shelter in case of attack. Businessmen took courses that taught them how to fight back if their plane was overtaken by hijackers. "Like it or not, we're all targets and we all need to become soldiers,"[41] said Walter Philbrick, a former SWAT instructor in Florida who taught a four-hour disaster preparedness class.

Most people tried to keep life as normal as possible. Adults who found themselves overly anxious signed up for yoga, massage, and stress reduction classes. Others turned to volunteer work. Parents emphasized family life, avoided news programs that might disturb their children, and assured their little ones that there were many people in the community—firefighters, police, and paramedics, for example—who would protect and care for them if the need arose.

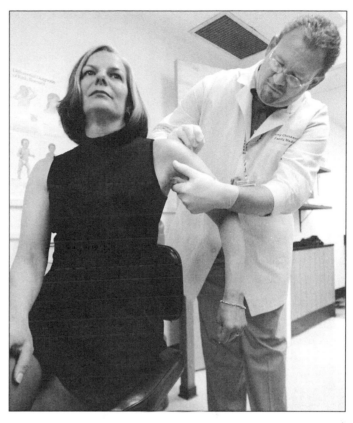

A woman receives a smallpox vaccination in 2003. Hospitals stockpiled vaccines in anticipation of a possible bioterrorist attack.

Homeland Security

While the private sector did what it could to prepare for a terrorist attack, the government worked to protect the nation in a broader sense. The Office of Homeland Security had been created by President Bush on October 8, 2001, in response to the September 11 attacks in New York and Washington, D.C. Bush appointed Governor Tom Ridge as head of the office, which became a cabinet-level post on January 24, 2003.

Homeland Security consolidated twenty-two previously separate agencies so that almost two hundred thousand people, ranging from biologists to border agents, worked together to guard against and prepare for a potential terrorist incident. Some of the diverse groups under Homeland Security control included the U.S. Coast Guard; the National Bio-Weapons Defense Analysis Center; the U.S. Secret Service; and the National Communications System, which provides communications support to critical government systems during emergencies. Homeland Security was officially responsible for everything from guarding borders, beefing up transportation security, and coordinating national emergency preparedness to protecting critical infrastucture such as bridges and tunnels and analyzing threats and intelligence.

At first, many Americans were skeptical that the new department would be able to operate effectively. They guessed that its size, complexity, and tight budget, would make it nonfunctional. They pointed out that not only did Ridge have to deal with terrorism, he also had to deal with acts of God—natural disasters such as floods, hurricanes, and earthquakes—because the Federal Emergency Management Agency reported to him as well. "The . . . obstacles to integrating these agencies are absolutely overwhelming,"[42] observed University of Pennsylvania criminologist Lawrence Sherman.

Despite the concerns, the new department got busy suggesting and launching improvements in many areas. Starting in May 2002, better-trained federal screeners checked passengers at a growing number of airports. Bulletproof, attack-proof cockpit doors kept pilots safer. Air marshals, alert for trouble, rode on many commercial flights. Bomb detection machines, devices that detect traces of explosives, and bomb-sniffing dogs were brought into many airports. Borders were better controlled after agreements were struck between Mexico, Canada, and the United States. Customs inspections were tightened. Power facilities were better patrolled.

Communication between the FBI and the CIA were improved. The FBI's outdated computer systems, which lacked Internet and e-mail capabilities, were upgraded. When completed, new systems were able to share information and images regarding potential terrorists and terrorist plots not only with the CIA but with the Pentagon; the Drug Enforcement Administration; the Bureau of Alcohol, Tobacco, Firearms and Explosives; and the State Department.

Alarming Accidents

Even with progress taking place, critics were quick to point out that there were still too many weaknesses in homeland security. Some of those weaknesses were highlighted as a result of accidents. In August 2003, for instance, a series of small power failures in northeast Ohio shut down a power grid and left 50 million people without electricity in the eastern United States and Canada. Thousands were stranded at work. Others were left without air conditioning and water. The blackout was not the result of terrorism, but people were troubled to learn that a vital system was so vulnerable. They wondered, too, what havoc terrorists could create if they invaded and shut down other vital systems, such as computer networks that controlled finances or nuclear power plants.

Other security weaknesses were highlighted by an act of a lone individual. In early 2004, for instance, letters containing the poison ricin were sent to Senate majority leader Bill Frist's office in Washington, D.C., causing disruption and alarm. No one fell ill, but the incident proved that the new radiation machines designed to kill deadly bacteria in post offices were not adequate protection. Poisons like ricin were unaffected by the radiation.

One of the most chilling illustrations of inadequate security took place in September 2003. That fall, Nathaniel Heatwole, a twenty-year-old college student, revealed that he had repeatedly breached security over an eight-month period at the Raleigh Durham International and Baltimore/Washington International airports. In each case, Heatwole had successfully carried suspicious items such as box cutters, bleach, clay molded to look like plastic explosives, and matches onto some commercial planes, hiding some of them in bathrooms. When the items were not discovered, Heatwole notified authorities, letting them know that his smuggling had been an "act of civil disobedience with the aim of improving public safety for the air-traveling public."[43]

Authorities ignored his communications. The objects were not noticed until a plumbing malfunction was reported on one of the planes five weeks later. When the connection was made to Heatwole, he was arrested, all the while insisting that he had carried out his activities solely to point out how easily terrorists could penetrate airport security.

Nathaniel Heatwole repeatedly breached security at two U.S. airports to prove how easily terrorists could target air traffic.

Holes in Security

College student Nathaniel Heatwole's deliberate breach of airline security in September 2003 was not the only incident where airport defense proved inadequate. In "Bumps in the Sky," published in *Time* magazine, authors Daren Fonda and Sally B. Donnelly give an overview of several other eye-opening episodes.

No one with a deep understanding of aviation security thinks we're safe enough. [Nathaniel] Heatwole was hardly the first guy to pull off an outlandish security breach in recent months. In September [2003] a New York City man had himself packed in a crate and shipped to Dallas in the cabin of a cargo plane and remained undetected through four airports. In August at New York City's JFK airport, three fishermen whose raft was caught in choppy waters tied it to a pier, walked onto a runway and wandered around for nearly an hour past jets with people on board before stumbling upon the airport's police headquarters. Local airports and law enforcement bear some responsibility for those breaches. But if they are so easy for amateurs and bumblers, how tough would they be for the criminally minded?

Not Good Enough

In May 2002 the insecurity of the nation's ports was illustrated when the news revealed that twenty-five Islamic extremists might have entered the United States by hiding in shipping containers. More than seven thousand ships make over fifty thousand stops in U.S. ports each year. Those ports are usually located in highly populated areas, near refineries that produce highly volatile petrochemicals and convert crude oil into gasoline and heating oil. In

2002, most were inadequately guarded. The volume of traffic going through them allowed terrorists opportunities to smuggle themselves or their weapons into the country with little risk of detection. "A terrorist attack launched on or at our ports could shut down commerce for days or weeks and could have immense costs,"[44] said Senator Patty Murray of Washington State.

Port security had been upgraded somewhat since September 11, but progress was too slow, critics insisted, and only the largest ports were being improved. Ships, ports, ferry terminals, and fuel depots needed to submit security plans showing how they would deal with a potential terrorist threat. New technology needed to be added to detect radioactivity, a sign of a dirty bomb, which, if set off in a public place, could expose large numbers of Americans to deadly radiation. Sea marshals needed to be aboard all ships entering U.S. ports to prevent hijackings. Ships needed to be required to provide electronic information about cargoes twenty-four hours before they embarked for U.S. ports so agents could target those that might be dangerous. Customs agents needed to screen cargo using high-tech tools such as X-ray scanners. "I think we all know that terrorists are terribly creative and ingenious and are determined and we have to do everything we can to stop them,"[45] Murray said.

All such changes cost money, and critics argued that too little had been allocated to help ports, airports, and other vital systems to upgrade and protect themselves. Money also needed to be spent to hire more and better security personnel, and to pay them better so they would be highly motivated and make fewer mistakes. Due to poor security, illegal immigrants still sneaked across U.S. borders regularly. People with knives were getting aboard flights unhindered. One woman boarded a US Airways flight to Philadelphia in late 2003 carrying a six inch kitchen knife for cutting an apple she had brought as a snack. Cargo containers that were supposed to be empty were not checked, although they could easily carry contraband.

Ridge defended his office and his subordinates, highlighting the fact that with a country as large as the United States to protect, neither training nor money could close the millions of security gaps that were bound to occur annually. Budget director Mitchell Daniels supported Ridge's position. "There is not enough money in the galaxy to protect . . . every American against every

In March 2003 a Coast Guard vessel escorts an oil barge from port at New Haven, Connecticut.

conceivable threat that every hateful fanatic in the world might conjure up."[46]

A Question of Rights

At the same time that many Americans wanted stricter homeland security, others worried that tougher security policies would compromise their civil liberties too much. Most agreed that increased security was necessary. Nevertheless, they were wary of those who seemed eager to restrict liberties for the good of the country. Mary Jo White, a former U.S. attorney in New York, said, "There is a significant civil-liberties price to be paid as we adopt various national-security initiatives. For the most part I think that price is necessary. But what I worry about is government officials who find the answers too easy in this arena."[47]

Some of those who were asked to sacrifice most when it came to civil liberties were people of Middle Eastern descent. In the days after September 11, and then again as the United States went to war in Iraq, these individuals were scrutinized particularly closely as they went through security checks in buildings, airports, and the like. Many Iraqi Americans were interviewed by FBI agents who came to their homes and asked them to voluntarily supply answers to questions such as "Do you support Saddam Hussein?" "Do you know any Saddam sympathizers?" "What is your religious affiliation?" and "What are the names and addresses of your Iraqi family members living in the United States?"

Some who were questioned saw the process as embarrassing or humiliating.

They were being targeted not because they had done anything wrong, but simply because of their ethnicity. Some were angry when a loved one who was judged suspicious was taken away and detained for an indefinite period of time.

Most cooperated willingly, however. They viewed their participation as their contribution to the country. They were even surprised and gratified to find that they were not required to answer the FBI's questions. In Iraq, failure to cooperate with the government usually meant imprisonment or death. "I think within the Arab-American community there are many people who worry about civil liberties and persecution," said Subhi, a graduate student at Rice University in Texas. "But I was basically eager to let them know our story. I didn't want them to have doubts or questions about our status, and I wanted to resolve any questions they might have. We have nothing to hide as Iraqis."[48]

Governmental Power

There were some Americans who felt that targeting Iraqi Americans was intolerable. They pointed out that other acts such as jailing asylum seekers from Muslim nations and Haiti (a route for illegal immigration), classing those suspected of terrorist ties as "enemy combatants" rather than prisoners of war (POWs), and denying them the rights that POWs were accorded under the Geneva Convention was wrong as well. Some of these rights include humane treatment, protection against acts of violence

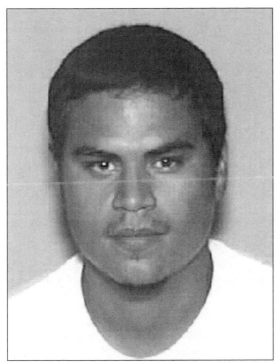

José Padilla, a suspected al Qaeda operative, was held in prison for two years without regular access to a lawyer.

or intimidation, and protection against public insults and abuse.

Particularly disturbing to them were cases like that of José Padilla, a U.S. citizen who was accused in 2002 of being an al Qaeda operative who planned to detonate a "dirty" bomb contaminated with radioactive elements in the United States. Classed as an enemy combatant, Padilla remained in prison without being charged with a crime and without regular access to a lawyer for almost two years before the Supreme Court heard his case. "It's finally time for the basic questions about the scope

of the president's power to hold people without the approval of the courts . . . to be confronted,"[49] said Thomas Goldstein, an appellate attorney who argued dozens of cases before the high court.

Americans who criticized the government's handling of the Padilla case also believed that the government was infringing on Americans' civil liberties in other ways. They cited the USA PATRIOT Act, passed by Congress on October 25, 2001, which removed restraints on law enforcement and allowed the FBI to access private medical records, library records, student records, and other background information in an effort to identify terrorists.

Librarians were among those who protested the new freedoms the Patriot Act gave law enforcement officials. Dedicated to the free and open exchange of knowledge and information, they saw the act as a gross violation of individuals' privacy rather than an enhancement of investigatory tools that could block terrorist acts. Thus, when told by the government that they might be required to turn over patrons' library records to help identify potential terrorists, some rebelled. At the end of each day, they deleted the names of patrons who used computers, thus eliminating any records the FBI could use. They also posted signs in the library, warning patrons that the government might access their records. "People expect that what they use at the library is nobody else's business," said Elliot Shelkrot, director of a Philadelphia library. "If they can all of a sudden have their records examined because of some allegation, it presents a situation where Big Brother is watching you."[50]

The Rule of Reason

While Americans like Shelkrot worried about violations of civil liberties, others brushed off such fears as overreactions. Compromises were sometimes necessary during war, especially when many people could suffer unless protective steps were taken. For instance, President Abraham Lincoln had suspended the right of habeas corpus, a safeguard against unlawful imprisonment, during the Civil War. According to former attorney general of the United States William Barr, compromise was simple common sense. He noted, "Where you are dealing with extraordinary threats that could take tens of thousands of lives, a rule of reason has to prevail."[51]

Barr also believed the Patriot Act was necessary in modern times when mobile phones, computers, and air travel made it easier than ever for terrorists to operate. It merely strengthened law enforcement's ability to go after terrorists by allowing information sharing as well as increased surveillance of suspected terrorists. He noted that "the danger to our civil liberties comes from the terrorists . . . not the government's actions. I think the government's actions have been restrained, moderate, well within the law and pose no genuine civil liberties concerns."[52]

Another tool applauded by supporters of the Patriot Act was the Computer Assisted Passenger Prescreening System II

New Powers

In a 2001 article entitled "Justice Department Begins New Anti-Terrorist Measures," found on the Web site The Tech, journalist Josh Meyer interprets some of the sweeping new powers the PATRIOT Act gave the Justice Department. Many Americans fear the act could erode the constitutional and civil rights of those who are suspected of terror in the future.

Intelligence information on suspected terrorists that was previously off-limits to FBI agents will be handed over to them so they can begin building criminal cases.

Special "roving" wiretaps, which follow an individual rather than a phone number, will be put in place, and expanded search warrants prepared and executed.

Authorities will pursue a dramatically broadened list of terrorism-related crimes. In many cases, authorities will be able to hold suspects in custody for longer periods, in an effort to link them to suspected terrorist plots.

Agents will pursue suspected terrorists into the darkest corners of cyberspace, taking advantage of new subpoena power to obtain previously prohibited information about their credit cards and bank account numbers.

And information obtained through grand jury subpoenas will be shared with other law enforcement authorities, loosening the secrecy that has long surrounded the federal indictment process, according to senior Justice Department officials.

(CAPPS II)—a process whereby airport security agents could review a person's identity, financial and commercial information, and criminal record when that person booked a seat on an airliner. Expected to be tested in 2004, the system could look for hints of security risks and help stop terrorists before they struck. Passengers would be "color coded"—green passengers would be risk-free, yellows would need further screening and reds would be too dangerous to allow aboard a plane.

Civil libertarians insisted that accessing innocent individuals' files was another invasion of privacy and should not be tolerated. They also feared that the process could be misused. "This system threatens to create a permanent blacklisted underclass of Americans who cannot travel freely,"[53] said Katie Corrigan, a lawyer with the American Civil Liberties Union, an organization that guards civil rights.

Law enforcement officials, on the other hand, insisted that they needed every tool they could get to catch terrorists who used weakness in America's surveillance systems to help achieve their aims. They applauded the CAPPS program and other advancements such as the establishment of the Terrorist Screening Center, where twelve federal "watch lists" of terrorist suspects were merged into one for easier access. Located in Washington, D.C., the center is administered by the FBI. Another agency known as the Terrorist Threat Integration Center helped coordinate all threat-related information that came into different agencies in the United States. It then ensured that information was analyzed and acted on as quickly as possible.

The issue of civil liberties versus national security remained a hot topic with Americans into 2004. To moderates, it seemed like law enforcement and the government had to constantly negotiate a delicate balance—not overstepping their authority but doing enough to prevent a devastating terrorist attack. Law enforcement officials acknowledged that the decisions they made constantly required compromise and creativity. "We're making this up as we go along," said one FBI official. "It's a brave new world out there."[54]

Their efforts and mistakes were always exposed to public scrutiny by the media, which provided nonstop coverage of the war on any given day. As with any issue, some Americans appreciated the coverage, others viewed it with skepticism. Few denied the influence it had on the nation's perception of itself, its leaders, and the war, however. "The power of the media to set a nation's agenda . . . is an immense and well-documented influence," observed expert Maxwell McCombs. "What we know about the world is based largely on what the media decides to tell us."[55]

Chapter 3

The War and the Media

In the spring of 2003, Americans saw the war in Iraq unfold on their television screens. The news—often on the air twenty-four hours a day, seven days a week—presented the conflict in real time and in living color. Everyone watched as troops advanced into Iraq; battled monumental desert sandstorms; fought the enemy near towns like Umm Qasr, An-Nasiriya, and Al-Musaib; and made their entry into Baghdad on April 7.

The media helped the nation focus on war. They also sparked innumerable questions and criticisms from those who believed that reporters and news commentators were too much of a factor in the conflict. Despite all the coverage, Americans were not seeing the war firsthand. Rather, their knowledge of events, progress, and decisions made by the government and the military was filtered through the network they watched. Stories could be discarded, edited, played up or played down, all at the discretion of a news editor. That seemed risky. Anchorman and columnist Bill O'Reilly pointed out that "Americans are still distrustful of the media they depend upon for vital information. A [2003] Gallup Poll says 60% of Americans believe the media are biased; 45% think the media too liberal, 15% say too conservative."[56]

Media Bias

Newspersons were supposed to be objective in the way they covered the war, and most tried as hard as possible to present their reports in a balanced way. Each unwittingly conveyed his or her own personal slant, however, simply by the words that were chosen and the way the story was told. Often this was done in so subtle a way that it was hard to notice. For instance, *New York Times* reporter David Chen wrote at the start of the war: "New Yorkers watching the televised bombing of Baghdad yesterday said they were riveted by the raw and uninterrupted display of American military might. But for some, the bombing brought back particularly visceral and chilling memories. They could not help thinking about Sept. 11, and how New York, too, was once under assault from the skies."[57] The use of the words "raw," "chilling," and "assault" were prone to conjure up negative rather than positive emotions in the reader, and the comparison of the bombing of Baghdad to terror attacks of September 11, implied that the two incidents were equally unjustified.

A variety of other factors in addition to personal bias made media objectivity virtually impossible as well. Loyalty—

specifically to the news network they worked for—was one factor. For instance, Fox News was owned by media mogul Rupert K. Murdoch, known to be conservative. Ted Turner, who was more liberal, owned CNN. The outlook of both men influenced not only the people they hired, but the stories that were reported on their networks, and the tone of the reporting. Fox News was known to have a conservative slant—for

A journalist reports from the entrance to the hole in Tikrit in which Saddam was hiding when he was captured in December 2003.

instance, broadcasting stories that portrayed antiwar protesters in an unflattering light—while CNN might portray those protesters more sympathetically.

A study done by the Center for Media and Public Affairs, a research and educational organization that conducts scientific studies of the news, showed that other news agencies had pronounced slants to their coverage, too. Of the three American network news stations, ABC was found to be the most critical of the war, with two out of three on-air comments negative. CBS's coverage was the most supportive, with nearly three out of every four opinions favorable. NBC was most balanced—53 percent positive versus 47 percent negative. Because most Americans usually watched one channel more than the others, they were likely to get a biased view of the war. Media director Matthew Felling noted, "Unless they have six eyeballs and a lot of time, they can't watch all the networks. They are more likely to watch the same network consistently; so if they are watching only ABC, they are seeing more negative coverage and if they are watching only CBS, they are seeing more positive coverage."[58]

Biased Which Way?

Although most Americans agreed with critics that the news was biased, they had differing opinions on the slant that bias took. Conservatives in particular were convinced that the media were biased in a liberal way. They pointed to news stories that drew attention to civil rights abuses and antiwar demonstrations—both liberal causes—as proof of that stance.

They also noted the media's tendency to question and criticize military and government leadership, to emphasize that the war was not going as planned, to assert that Iraqi people despised the military, and to imply that a humanitarian disaster was looming in Iraq. *Newsweek* Washington Bureau Chief Evan Thomas stated, "There is a liberal bias. It's demonstrable. You look at some statistics. About 85 percent of the reporters who cover the White House vote Democratic, they have for a long time. There is a, particularly at the networks, at the lower levels, among the editors and the so-called infrastructure, there is a liberal bias."[59]

Not so, other Americans countered. In this war, the media were a tool of the administration, unthinkingly repeating what government and military spokesmen told them. Reporters did not question authority, and often exhibited overt pride and patriotism when talking about the military and what it was doing. Anchormen and commentators such as Sean Hannity of Fox News uninhibitedly showed their pleasure when American sentiments echoed their own. For instance, in citing a December 2003 Gallup poll, Hannity said: "Fifty-nine percent of Americans get it, that we had to do it [go to war in Iraq]. They support the president. It was the right thing to do."[60]

Critics also noted a proadministration bias in the way American media chose not

Middle Eastern Perspective

News bias is apparent when American coverage is compared to Al Jazeera and other Middle Eastern media stations. As James Poniewozik reported in a *Time* magazine article entitled "What You See vs. What They See," different cultures focus on different aspects of the war when they report the news.

> Like US TV, the Arab networks show briefings, sound bites from George W. Bush and Tony Blair, allied advances and even interviews with coalition troops. . . . But they also show charred bodies lying beside gutted cars. Cameras linger over dead allied soldiers and bandaged Iraqi children. Mourning families wail, and hospitals choke with bleeding and burned civilians. If the war on American TV has been a splendid fireworks display and tank parade punctuated by press conferences, on al-Jazeera et al., war is hell. . . .

> Western and Arab media are driven by the same imperative—to feed the hunger for human interest. Their interests are simply in different humans. . . . History will have to sort out many points on which Western and Middle Eastern TV differ: how effective the allied war effort is, how warmly Iraqis will receive its results, and which media are more accurate and neutral. What we do know is that war is a horrible thing in which people die horribly. So far, there is no question which networks own that story.

to broadcast as many graphic scenes of death and violence as did foreign media. Such scenes were bound to disturb viewers and turn some against the conflict. Reporters seldom challenged the rightness of the war, either, as did reporters in other countries. Journalism professor Robert Jenson observed:

> The U.S. media did a good job of describing the lives of the military personnel and narrating the advance of U.S. troops, and a lousy job of covering the politics of the war. Readers and listeners all over the world were exposed to a vigorous discussion of the motivations behind the war, but Americans—especially those who got their news from television—were largely deprived of that reporting and analysis.[61]

Drama and Excitement

Financial considerations also impacted the way the media reported the news. "The media industry operates to realize a profit for its owners/stockholders, not necessarily to make the world a better place by keeping its readers, or in this case viewers, informed,"[62] stated media specialist James Tracey.

Stories that were compelling and exciting attracted a wider audience, while stories that were newsworthy but boring sometimes led viewers to change the channel or stop reading the newspaper. Thus, news outlets worked as hard as possible to present the most interesting news in the most dramatic way. Reporters often did stories on bombings, protests, and children who had been wounded rather than covering water mains that had been rebuilt, roads

Images such as this one depicting grateful Kurds standing atop a toppled statue of Saddam were widely circulated by the American media.

that had been repaved, or villages where families had been untouched by the war. Representative Jim Marshall of Georgia observed after a trip to Iraq in September 2003, "They [the media] are dwelling upon the mistakes, the ambushes, the soldiers killed, the wounded. Fair enough. But it is not balancing this bad news with 'the rest of the story,' the progress made daily, the good news."[63]

Good news did get coverage if it was exciting enough. For instance, Iraqis who thronged the streets of Baghdad, embrac-

ing soldiers and toppling statues of Saddam on the day of his overthrow were top news stories for days. The triumphant rescue of Private Jessica Lynch was given thorough coverage on news networks as well. Lynch was one of nineteen soldiers who were captured by Iraqis on March 23 after taking a wrong turn near the town of Nassiriya. The capture made headlines in the United States after a photo of Specialist Shoshana Johnson, another female captive, was shown on Iraqi television. Footage of Johnson, Lynch, and other POWs united the nation in horror. "The mood on post is very tragic,"[64] stated spokeswoman Jean Offutt at Fort Bliss, Texas, where many of the POWs had been stationed.

Although there was little difference between Johnson's and Lynch's stories, Lynch became a media darling and a hero when the story of her dramatic rescue hit newspapers and airwaves nine days after her capture. People around the world absorbed all the details of the event, which had been recorded live on grainy green film carried by a combat camera crew. Pictures of the fragile looking teen who had been rescued by a squad of U.S. Army Rangers, Navy SEALS, marines, and air

force combat controllers were played for all to see. In the words of author Ellen Turkenich, "There were all the elements that create a good drama; the conflict, the human interest, the familiar and reassuring cast of characters, and the unforgettable villains, with a good dose of action to keep boys interested and emotional tearjerking scenes for the ladies."[65]

After her return to the United States, Lynch's celebrity continued. Her biography was published and a made-for-television movie about her ordeal aired. She rode in parades, received awards, and was invited to the Golden Globe telecast. In contrast, Johnson and six male POWs who

Jessica Lynch, pictured on parade in Palestine, West Virginia, became a media darling after she was rescued from captivity in Iraq.

were released and returned to the United States in April 2003 received less recognition, although all suffered injury and trauma during their POW experience. The media had its star in Lynch, so the others were portrayed without drama and fanfare.

What If . . .

In order to give their reports drama, newspersons often added elements of conjecture and speculation to the facts. For instance, when hearing that a government or military official was going to make an important announcement, a newsperson often explored the possibilities on-air of what the speaker might say. Or, after a speech was given or a policy change was announced, a news team would speculate about possible scenarios that might evolve out of that decision. Such educated guessing often included a "worst-case" possibility, which whetted the audience's curiosity and ensured that they would keep watching the news to see what developed.

Conjecture and speculation sometimes led to mistaken reporting, however. In one case, for example, a newsperson reported that Secretary of Defense Donald Rumsfeld had not seen an important memo stating that National Security Advisor Condoleezza Rice's department would be taking a larger role in coordinating operations in Iraq. Because Rumsfeld's Department of Defense had led the operation thus far, and because Rumsfeld had not read the memo, the newsperson speculated that the secretary was being pushed out of

war leadership. In fact, the truth was more mundane. The secretary had not been slighted or ignored, he had simply been busy. His staff had read and noted the memo, just as they did with other similar communications.

News based on speculation could and did affect public opinion, as when the media speculated about whether the United States was going to become "bogged down" in Iraq as it had in the Vietnam War. News analysts listed points of comparison including the growing number of American deaths, the upsurge in guerrilla warfare, and the declining popularity of Bush as compared to President Lyndon Johnson.

The speculation stirred up the fears of those who remembered that earlier conflict all too well. Above all, they did not want to get caught up in a scenario similar to the one they had lived through in the 1960s and 1970s. Even retired marine general Anthony Zinni, who served in Vietnam, was alarmed. "We saw the sacrifice, and we swore never again would we allow it to happen. And I ask you, is it happening again?"[66]

Those who knew all the facts were able to somewhat counter the worries. Retired air force lieutenant general Tom McInerney visited Iraq in late 2003, and stated, "The fact is, the media has got it all wrong. The situation there is far better than people realize."[67] Nevertheless, the fear that the war could become a "quagmire" helped weaken public resolve to remain involved in the conflict.

Avoiding a Quagmire

To some Americans, the war in Iraq bore a disturbing resemblance to the war in Vietnam with its high casualty rate and unwinnable strategy. In an article entitled "Why Iraq Is Not like Vietnam," published online at the *Christian Science Monitor* Web site, journalist John Hughes explores how the U.S. government could avoid repeating mistakes that sent it into the 1960s military quagmire.

> The fact is there are many dissimilarities between Vietnam and Iraq. The Vietnam War was fought in rice paddies and difficult jungle terrain. The continuing conflict in Iraq is confined mainly to the urban areas. . . . In Vietnam, the US was defending a people whose government was often corrupt and unloved. In Iraq, the US is seeking to defend a people who already have been liberated from a despotic regime.

> There is, however, one striking similarity between Vietnam and Iraq, namely the goals and strategy of the guerrillas attacking US forces. . . . In Iraq, as it was in Vietnam, the aim of the guerrillas is to undermine US resolve to the point where the US withdraws its forces, awarding the guerrillas the victory they could not win on the battlefield. . . .

> So what must happen to keep a quagmire for the US in Iraq from becoming reality? First, support at home for the US effort in Iraq must not weaken. . . . Second, security must improve. That requires more Iraqi policemen, and more international troops for peacekeeping, which is no long-term task for US and British combat units. . . . Finally, Iraqis must step up to their responsibilities. It is their country to build and to democratize. In eliminating Hussein's evil grasp, the US has given them a new opportunity. It is theirs to seize or lose.

Worry and Fear

Some who viewed the media critically pointed out that they had more serious faults than simple bias or faulty speculation. First, critics pointed to the growing tendency to show shocking or explicit photos of the war. American networks were restrained in comparison to Middle Eastern networks that carried images of mutilated children, the beheading of hostages, and the like, but some American editors believed that audiences should be allowed to see the ugliness of the conflict firsthand. Thus they had begun to show still photos of corpses and even the faces of Iraqi prisoners of war. The former was immoral according to some, and the latter was a debatable act under the terms of the Geneva Convention. "These images were necessary to show an important aspect of the conflict," Tony Maddox of CNN International stated, referring to his network's decision to broadcast photos of dead American soldiers. "It's important to let the audience form its own view."[68]

Those who supported the move pointed out that with limitless access to the Internet, Americans could see such images at any time with just the click of a button. Nevertheless, critics pointed out that issues of taste, decency, and merit needed to be taken into consideration when decisions to air such photos on television were made.

A second fault of the media was their tendency to relay information to the public too quickly. That haste was based in part on a time-honored principle—"the public's right to know." Being the first to break a story was also profitable, however, since it attracted more viewers. Certain information such as troop movements and battle plans were usually respected as classified, but everything else was likely to be published or broadcast. Americans worried about the broadcast of information that might be helpful to the enemy.

Their concerns seemed reasonable, given the facts. Since the beginning of the war on terror, potentially dangerous information had been published several times. In one instance, a CNN report on January 17, 2002, listed several large cities in the United States as being the most poorly prepared for a terrorist attack. The information in effect told terrorists where an attack could be most effective. In March 2002 the *Los Angeles Times* published a story about the United States's nuclear policy and the countries it viewed as threats. Critics pointed out that listing such nations in time of war could perhaps lead to a wider outbreak of hostilities. In yet another instance, in late March 2003 television correspondent Geraldo Rivera sketched the 101st Airborne Division's battle plans in the sand while on the air. His employer, Fox News, immediately ordered him back to Kuwait.

Newspersons did not agree that such articles and broadcasts posed any threat to U.S. security. They insisted that any information a journalist could access was probably available to terrorists as well. "If a terrorist wants to know who to attack, they'll do their own research and find out on their own. Our reporting isn't going to tip them off,"[69] journalist Mike Fish said. At the same time, good could sometimes come of such reporting. For instance, the article on weak security in U.S. cities focused public attention on those locales. As a result, improvements were made.

Despite the media's assertions, at least one time when reporters quickly broadcast information without considering its impact, panic ensued. In a press conference in February 2003, just after the terror alert level had been raised to orange (high danger), an official from the Federal Emergency Management Agency mentioned to reporters that Americans would be wise to have emergency kits including rolls of duct tape and plastic sheeting to seal off rooms and doors in case of a biochemical attack. Reporters found the information interesting and dramatic and highlighted it in the news. The next day, programs such as *Good Morning America* were showing people how to designate a "safe" room in the house and make it airtight.

Conscientious Americans took the advice and rushed to buy necessary supplies. The news was soon reporting that shortages of duct tape and plastic sheeting were occurring in some locales. This sparked panic. More people rushed to the store, and the shortages became more widespread. The furor did not die down until Homeland Security secretary Tom Ridge revised the message and urged calm. He stated, "I want to make something very, very clear at this point: We do not want individuals or families to start sealing their doors or their windows."[70] Experts also pointed out that sealing a room completely could even be dangerous because all fresh air would be cut off and anyone inside would slowly suffocate to death.

Change of Policy

With the power of the media broadly recognized during the war, the Defense Department decided to enact a change in policy. This change gave newspeople greater access to the war while still controlling their movements. The department had tried to

In February 2003 a Virginia woman buys a roll of plastic sheeting to help protect her home from chemical attack.

ignore or block the efforts of reporters since the Vietnam War, when news reports had been universally critical of the military. Other incidents, like one in Somalia in 1992 when marines made a nighttime landing on the beach only to be met by journalists, floodlights, and camera crews, had deepened the department's distrust of the media's good judgment.

During the Persian Gulf War in 1991, reporters' movements had been highly restricted by the military. Photos, news footage, and battlefield dispatches had to be cleared with military officials before they were released to the public. Some news organizations even filed lawsuits charging the military with violating the First Amendment guarantee of freedom of the press. Rear Admiral John Bitoff explained the military's position by citing national security. He said: "There is a clear and present danger in today's instant-communications age, which

An embedded journalist assigned to a military unit in central Iraq uses his jacket to protect his computer as he works.

may put our troops at risk. Our enemies are watching CNN-TV."[71]

In order to satisfy both sides, in 2003 the Defense Department came up with the strategy of "embedding." One or two reporters were assigned to live and travel with a military unit, and could report and photograph events from a firsthand point of view. Some members of the military were skeptical, believing that the embed, as the reporter was called, would get in the way and might even be killed. Still, the experiment seemed worth a try.

To many people's surprise, embedding proved not only workable, but also popular with the audience, the military, and journalists. With about five hundred reporters in the field, television viewers were able to get exciting, immediate information. Reporters no longer had to fight for access to information. Everything that happened to a unit could be recorded, from the chaos of battle to the letdown after a fight. (Reporters agreed not to broadcast the location and size of military units or identify the wounded and dead before the military could notify their next of kin.) NBC correspondent Chip Reid, embedded with the Third Battalion, Fifth Marine Regiment, recalled, "I can't think of a time when we were flatly denied access. We were sometimes even given military plans in advance—to help us plan our coverage. It didn't take long for the Marines to learn that they could trust us and for us to learn that we could rely on them."[72]

Online Censorship

Television and newspapers often censored themselves during the war in Iraq to avoid leaking information to the enemy or offending the public. An article entitled "POW Pictures Spark Internet Censorship Debate" published on the *USA Today* Web site, demonstrated that even online information, which is not traditionally censored, could be blocked in the cause of patriotism. Photos of POWs are viewed by most Americans as exploitive and in bad taste.

A Florida-based Web hosting company knocked a small news site offline after it posted controversial photos of captured American soldiers, stoking accusations that private firms are censoring free speech. . . .

U.S. television networks had been abiding by a U.S. Pentagon request not to show the footage. "I think we were the first Web site to show the images. . . . But the site was down a few hours later, without any warning." . . .

Vortech [the server] . . . cited viewer complaints and argued the images constituted a breach of the firm's usage agreements. . . . "No TV station in the U.S. is allowing any dead U.S. soldiers or POWs to be displayed and we will not either. We understand free press and all but we don't want someone's family member to see them on some site. It is disrespectful, tacky and disgusting," read the e-mail explanation.

"Searchlight in a Dark Room"

Embedded reporters and round-the-clock cable news reporting gave everyone uninterrupted access to war events. Military experts in the news studios used maps and graphs to make situations more understandable. Analysts dissected every event, giving multiple opinions about the significance

An embedded reporter (right) eats with his unit. The camaraderie some reporters developed with their units threatened to cloud their ability to report with objectivity.

of military maneuvers. Many Americans felt better informed than ever before.

There were those who disagreed, however. Analysts and experts were good, but embedding had potential weaknesses that could seriously affect the public's perception of the war. For example, although embeds got a thorough feel for people and events in their unit, their perspective of the overall war was extremely limited. They could report only on events they witnessed. This sometimes resulted in lack of perspective. Jamie Cowling, a research fellow at the Institute of Public Policy Research in London, added, "It's comparable to a searchlight in a dark room rather than being able to turn the lights full on."[73]

Embedded reporters often developed friendly relationships with their units, making true objectivity even more difficult. The embed traveled, ate, and shared all the hardships of war with the soldiers. He or she admired their courage and sacrifice, became close friends with some of them, and even came to identify with them. Critics asked, Could a newsperson report objectively in such a situation? If the unit made mistakes or acted wrongly, perhaps the reporter would not report them. If unit commanders presented a situation in a biased way, the reporter might accept it as the whole truth instead of making an effort to get opposing views.

Supporters of embedding pointed out that reporters might not be totally unbiased, but at least they were reporting what they actually saw. They were not relying on military or government spokespeople who had their own subjective points of view. Also, embeds were generally professional enough to ignore their feelings about the unit they accompanied. Many exhibited that objectivity by filing reports that were not flattering to the troops. For instance, Reid reported an instance of civilian casualties when the men of his unit mistakenly killed two young Iraqi girls during a night battle. He faced criticism after making the report, but stood firm on his principles. "After I reported it a couple of Marines asked me why I had put it on the air. They said it would make the Marines look bad. They were surprised, they said, because they thought I was their 'friend.' They even asked me whose side I was on."[74]

Recognizing the power and influence the media had in the United States, some military families turned to it when they had a specific need relating to a relative overseas. For instance, when Shoshana Johnson was captured, her family allowed itself to be interviewed several times in order to keep her face in the public and her return a top national priority. "I realized media attention is the thing that brought that girl [Elizabeth Smart] home,"[75] said Margaret Thorne-Henderson, Johnson's aunt, referring to the kidnapped Utah girl who had been returned to her family in March 2003.

Other military families just watched the news avidly, always on the lookout for a glimpse of a loved one. Being an American during the war in Iraq was not easy. Being left behind to cope with life while a husband, wife, son, or daughter fought overseas created some extra challenges. Twenty-two-year-old Nina Berger observed, "It's been tough: worrying about my husband, paying the bills and taking care of the kids. I wish he was here, but he's got a job to do. [So] right now, I've got to be a mother and a father."[76]

Chapter 4

Heroes at Home

To Americans on the home front, the young men and women who served overseas were heroes working to bring peace and order to Iraq. A second group of heroes were not so squarely in the public eye, however. These were the families of those who served, and their sacrifice was significant, as Patricia Erickson, daughter of a veteran, explained:

> While military personnel might be recognized at a parade or admired for the medals they wear honoring their service, the contribution that is often overlooked is the one made by the military family. They sacrifice time spent with their spouse or parent during deployments, they sacrifice friendships and a stable home life each time they move across country, and they sacrifice peace of mind because they love someone in a dangerous occupation.[77]

Sacrifices

Military families were always vulnerable to the fears and hardships that came with war. Daily routines were broken when a loved one was deployed. Children went without one or both parents for months at a time. Parents worried about sons and daughters. Spouses became single parents, coping with work, schoolwork, and responsibilities that ranged from paying bills to dealing with home repairs.

Despite the difficulties, most insisted that the sacrifice was important and worthwhile. In their view, serving one's country was one of the most important responsibilities an American could shoulder. They were as patriotic as any soldier overseas, and felt proud to be able to do their part, even if that was as mundane as keeping the family and household in good shape so their loved one would have someplace to come home to. "Of course, the biggest effect is loneliness," said Diana Gundersen, whose husband Ed was overseas during the Iraq War. "I've got two children; they're teenagers. It's been difficult, but it's not been impossible."[78]

A Time for Courage

Every military family developed its own way of dealing with a loved one's absence. Many kept the television turned off for fear that what they heard would be disturbing. Others watched the news to keep abreast of current events. "I'm terrified of what I might see and yet I find it impossible to turn the television off while my husband is fighting this war,"[79] said Denise Gonsales, whose husband served in Iraq.

Letters and phone calls overseas were infrequent, short, and unsatisfying, but e-mail messages were helpful to both those who served in Iraq and those at home. In this way, news could be shared, lessening the loneliness on both sides of the ocean. Not everything could be communicated, however. Wives in particular chose not to share problems such as illness or a child's misbehavior because they were afraid that extra worries could distract their husbands from the dangerous work they faced. "If they're on a truck and they're not paying attention to their job because they're worried about their family, then someone can get hurt,"[80] said Connie DiCola of Colorado.

A soldier says good-bye to his family before being deployed to Iraq in February 2004.

One of the best ways to cope was to keep busy. Most took part in school and church activities. Support groups were helpful as well. Many of these were sponsored by the military or organizations like the Red Cross. Others were more informal. Service wife Ann Wray described her neighborhood situation: "There are five of us living next to each other. We go jogging together and meet every evening in someone's house. Wednesdays are Taco nights."[81]

Families had to work harder to keep their spirits high when hopes for a quick end to the war faded. Deployments were extended because the bulk of available troops were serving in Afghanistan and the Middle East and there were no replacements to call in. "The Army is stretched out and on the verge of being overextended,"[82] said Representative John Spratt, a Democrat from South Carolina.

Those at home had to learn to live with disappointment when six-month stints of service were extended to a year and sometimes longer. Babies were born, children graduated, anniversaries came and went, and holiday celebrations were put off. "I was hoping for something around Christmas," said Jennifer Mylott, who learned her husband would not return before May 2004. "It would have been a nice Christmas present to have him home."[83]

There were short periods of happiness for some. Soldiers who had served one year

Strong and Supportive

Most military spouses accept the stress and responsibility that go along with having loved ones away serving their county. In a March 2003 *Newsweek* article entitled "I'm Afraid to Look, Afraid to Turn Away," Denise Gonsales details some of the challenges she has faced and is facing as the war continues.

It's a stressful time for my family. I'm eight months pregnant and my husband, Martin, a Black Hawk pilot based in Savannah, GA, has been in Kuwait for more than two months. Not surprisingly, I've been glued to the television, watching events unfold in this latest conflict, praying for my husband's safe return. As hard as it is to wait, it's not the first time I've done it and I suspect it won't be the last.

My first husband, who died three and a half years ago, was part of the 160th Special Operations unit deployed in 1993 to Somalia, where two Black Hawk helicopters were downed. Five of our dearest friends were killed during that mission. To my everlasting horror, I watched on CNN as the bodies of two of them were dragged through the streets of Mogadishu by a riotous crowd. . . . Once the military officially declared the soldiers' deaths, I had to deliver the terrible news to two of their wives. . . .

My heart just pours out to Iraqi families; as a mother, I can't imagine living with my two kids in a neighborhood that's being bombed. . . . And as terrified as I am for Martin, I can't imagine being an Iraqi wife whose husband is leaving to go fight the Americans. At least I know my husband has a fighting chance.

in Iraq were granted two weeks' leave beginning in September 2003. Most were able to go home and spend a few days with family. The time was just long enough to make returning to Iraq extremely difficult, however. "It's going to be worse than the first time. We already said goodbye once. I didn't think we'd have to say it again,"[84] said thirteen-year-old Ashlee Lindenberg when her father had to return to Iraq.

Hard Hit

Extended tours of duty often had the most serious repercussions for reservists and members of the National Guard, who not only were a homeland security force guarding airports and power plants, but also made up a large percentage of the soldiers in Iraq. As of January 2004, a record number—164,244—were on active duty overseas. Known as "citizen soldiers" because in civilian life they were lawyers, nurses, teachers, mechanics, business managers, and the like, they had originally signed up for the reserve primarily for educational benefits or to make extra money. All were patriotic, but few had expected to be called to active duty.

Reservists' families had not expected such a scenario either. And a family member's absence was especially difficult because they had not experienced routine separations as had the families of regular military personnel. They were also unused to thinking of their loved one in danger. "It's tremendously stressful for anyone," said Gloria Byrne, the wife of a reservist. "I

A reservist hugs her husband before leaving for Iraq. Few reservists expected to be called to active duty in Iraq.

will make it through this. But I miss my husband and I want my husband home when it's time for him to come home."[85]

Paula Rodriguez, whose father served with a cargo transportation company in Iraq, initially rebelled at the thought of him going overseas. "In the beginning, I was a little selfish, wondering, 'Why are they taking you? Why? Why? Why?' Then I finally realized, he knows what he is doing, and he'll come back."[86]

Economic Hardship

Many reservists' families were left short of money when their service member was called to active duty. The government paid them as military personnel, but an estimated one-third of reservists received less money than they did from their civilian jobs. The financial shortfall meant that spouses had to tighten their budgets at the same time as they faced other challenges.

Sometimes even budgeting and good management was not enough to make up for the loss of funds. In the case of reservist Frank Guerra's family in Bakersfield, California, a daughter's medical bills, Frank's one-thousand-dollar-per-month pay cut, and the cancellation of his health insurance policy combined to leave his family uninsured and short of money as they faced large medical bills. "I just don't know why . . . [his employer] took [the health insurance] away when she needed it the most, especially with Frank being at war, fighting for our freedom, not just mine, but theirs too," said Lilly Guerra, Frank's wife. "For them to take it away upset me very much."[87]

Ted Valentini's small business collapsed after he was sent to Iraq in 2003. Valentini's deployment to Afghanistan after September 11 had hurt his company—Tramco Mold, Inc.—which made molds for plastics and electronics. He borrowed more than ninety thousand dollars in an attempt to save it, but his second deployment—to Iraq—was more than the company could withstand. It failed in April 2003. "So 15 years of trying to build up ourselves financially, prepare for retirement and to save money for our kids' college, it's gone. . . . We have to start over,"[88] said Valentini's wife, Penny.

Employers were faced with difficulties, too, when coping with reservists going to war. Often those in small towns and rural areas were faced with a shortage of vital personnel, as when caregivers such as firefighters and nurses were called overseas. In some cases, the shortage was more widespread. In Alabama, for instance, both the Department of Corrections and the Department of Public Safety lost a significant number of men and women to the National Guard and the reserves, leaving the streets short of patrol officers and prisons short of guards. "There is most definitely a concern for the officers' safety, for the inmates' safety and really a concern for the public's safety," said prison spokesman Brian Corbett. "There are times where we have one corrections officer in a dorm supervising 200 inmates and more."[89]

Employers were required by law to hold a reservist's job open until his return, meaning that companies had to train and make do with temporary help. Many employers also tried to make up for reductions in salaries that reservists experienced when they were deployed. Paying that amount in addition to the costs of hiring temporary help was another drain on company finances.

Despite the hardships, most employers remained supportive of their reservist employees. "It's humbling when you think about what they go through," said Michael Plass of Motorola Communications Electronics in Columbia, Maryland. "We're honored and proud to support them while they support this country's mission."[90]

Saying Thank You

When other Americans learned that military families were suffering because of the war, they did what they could to help, too. Communities took up collections of money and food. Volunteers from churches and neighborhoods offered to help with everything from babysitting to changing flat tires.

Organizations such as CertifiChecks, a gift certificate resource center, joined with the United Service Organizations (USO), the Air Force Aid Society, and several other agencies to take donations so that military families could buy groceries and other necessities. Fisher House, an organization that supports those in need in the military,

Two wives of soldiers in Iraq fill a shopping cart with food donated to the National Guard in Dublin, Ohio.

also offered gift certificates that could be used to buy food and staples through military commissaries (grocery stores).

On state and national levels, government officials sponsored and passed bills that provided improved benefits to reservists. Commissary privileges were granted, pay raises approved, and benefits expanded. "It's our small way of saying thank you to these folks for the ultimate gift of freedom,"[91] said Pennsylvania House majority leader Sam Smith, who supported a measure that expanded the definition of veteran to include volunteers who serve in combat zones. This change allowed federally activated reservists to receive state veterans' benefits.

Bring Them Home

Although most military families coped well during the time that their loved one was overseas, some suffered bouts of severe depression. Some spouses decided that they no longer wanted to be a part of the military and left their marriages.

Some reservists' families experienced anger and resentment over what they saw as unfair differences in the way reservists and regular troops were treated. The regulars received better pay and benefits and were assigned shorter deployments because they were traditionally in more danger. In Iraq, however, reservists faced extreme danger, too, and they could be assigned to serve as long as two years. They received fewer benefits than regulars, and had to purchase their own necessities such as shav-

ing cream, toilet paper, gun-cleaning solution, and weapon lubricant.

At times, reservists lacked even basic equipment that was provided for regular units. For instance, some reservists were given protective vests that were missing the metal plates that deflected automatic-rifle rounds. Many called home and asked families to purchase the plates for them. "We're getting people locally who are deployed National Guard and parents, specifically, coming in and buying," said Don Budke, vice president of sales for Reliance Armor in Cincinnati, Ohio. "The military people don't want to advertise the fact that there are people doing this on their own."[92]

Faced with such perceived unfairness, some reservist families decided to take action. Families of the 129th Transportation Company from Kansas were so angry when they learned that their loved ones could be in Iraq for up to two years that they started the Web site www.129bringthemhome.com (later changed to www.129supportingour soldiers.com). On the site they set up a petition for readers to sign. It stated, "There are single parents, business owners, employees and new fathers in our unit. The reserve system is not designed to supplement the military for such an extended period of time."[93] Overnight, the petition garnered more than eight thousand signatures. It also caught the attention of the Pentagon, which soon gave the 129th a firm date for its return.

As time passed and numbers of casualties in Iraq grew, even some families of reg-

"Do Not Say That You Are Proud"

Families of reservists and National Guard troops often seriously resented the burden the war put on their lives. In the following letter, entitled "Do Not Say That You Are Proud of Me," an anonymous woman explains the reason for her bitterness. The entire letter can be found on the Military Families Speak Out Web site.

> My husband joined the National Guard trusting that he would not be taken from his career and home and sent to war except in a dire emergency. He is willing to sacrifice everything to defend the United States and our constitution, should that be necessary. But it is not necessary: the United States is not in the midst of an emergency that threatens its existence.

His life is now literally in the hands of the government, and my life is severely disrupted. The sacred trust that I, my husband, and all Americans had with our government has been destroyed. My life has been turned upside down not out of absolute necessity but rather to further the aims of a very few elite politicians. My husband has been ripped from his home not to fight a threat to our survival but to enrich a few powerful individuals. . . .

Please, if you know someone who is obligated to join the war, at home or as a soldier, do not offer your pride. Instead, express your sorrow at their personal situation, ask if you can help, and work to ensure that needless wars are never again started by our country.

ular enlisted men and women began to question the United States' involvement in the war. Wives like Michelle Isom, whose husband was overseas, emphasized that she was proud of troops who were helping the Iraqis by protecting them, providing medical care, and opening schools, but questioned whether that work was worth the sacrifice Americans were making. "We haven't found weapons of mass destruction, and we didn't have the backing of the United Nations, and now we're the ones there occupying a country that doesn't want us," she said. "We're going to support our guys, because they're our guys, but we're not sure what they're fighting for anymore."[94]

Bad News

At the same time that families waited and looked forward to happy reunions, they battled the fear that their loved ones might never return. Iraq seemed to be growing more dangerous every day. Gene Babbel, whose daughter was in Iraq, observed, "The president said the war was over so damn quick. Now that looks good politically. But it is not true. Those people (US GIs) are being hit or killed on a daily basis."[95]

One of the worst moments a family could experience was receiving notification that a son or daughter, or husband or wife, had been injured or killed in combat. The bad news was usually first broken by military representatives who called or visited the home. Those who discovered their loved one was not fatally injured were usually somewhat reassured and sat back to await more details. Those who learned of a death were devastated. Nothing could ease the pain of loss. "He told me not to

worry. No bullets were flying, he's in a Bradley [fighting vehicle]. And you know, 24 hours later, we don't have our son,"[96] remembered Allen Vandayburg of Mansfield, Ohio.

Each family had to get through that devastating time and recover in its own way, but there were some resources to help ease grief. The Tragedy Assistance Program for Survivors (TAPS) offered aid, including grief counseling referral, to those who suffered loss. The military provided a "death gratuity"—usually about $6,000—a tax-free

During a military funeral, a grieving family mourns the loss of a loved one killed in Iraq.

life insurance benefit of about $250,000, and a monthly stipend that included child support from the government.

Family readiness groups, tightly knit groups of military spouses who did everything in their power to ease the hard times, were also there to offer assistance. The groups received no pay and performed tasks that ranged from arranging funerals and visiting the wounded to babysitting and shopping. Although the work was difficult, it had its rewards. "I ultimately do it for my husband Joe, because I care about him," said Beth Anderson of Fort Campbell, Kentucky. "And it allows him to do his job and it allows other soldiers to do their jobs, to know that they're secure, that their families are secure."[97]

Unmet Needs

Learning a loved one had committed suicide was even more painful than learning he or she had been killed in combat. The knowledge that a soldier had been terribly depressed, distraught, or stressed in the last days of his life was haunting to those who were left behind.

Suicide was a significant problem in Iraq, particularly during the summer of 2003. Twenty-two soldiers took their own lives that year. That number was believed to be about 20 percent higher than in previous wars.

The suicides did not just rock families, at times an entire community could be affected by a death. Such was the case after army Private First Class Corey Small killed himself in Iraq in July 2003. Small's wife and four-year-old son not only bore the loss, they faced the disapproval of some in their town who believed that suicide was shameful or sinful. Others linked it to mental illness or moral weakness. That disapproval stung, especially when some members of the local American Legion who had planned to name their post after Small changed their minds after hearing of the

Exceptional Sacrifice

The death of National Guard troops and army reservists, who never expected to go to war, is devastating to family and friends. In a September 2003 article entitled "US Army Extends Tours of Guard and Reserve Troops," journalist Kate Randall gives a few details of one casualty, Darryl T. Dent. The complete article can be found on the World Socialist Web site.

Since the US invaded Iraq in March, 289 US troops have been killed, including 19 National Guard troops and 12 Army Reservists. One of these casualties, 21-year-old Darryl T. Dent, was buried at Arlington National Cemetery in Washington DC on Tuesday [September 9, 2003]. He was killed by a detonated explosive as he rode with about 20 members of the DC Army Guard's 547th Transportation Company in a convoy providing security for a mail run in the northern Iraqi city of Al Adsad.

Darryl Dent's story is similar to those of many men and women who signed up for the Guard or Reserves and found themselves in war-torn Iraq or Afghanistan, facing a population increasingly hostile to US military occupation. He joined the National Guard in 1999 and, before being deployed overseas in April, worked as a security guard in a mall in Arlington, Virginia.

According to Vernon Dent, the young man's father, Darryl dreamed of attending medical school and had no plans to make a career out of military service. The senior Dent reacted bitterly to his son's death and the news that other young men and women would be kept overseas longer. "What they [the government] need to do," he told the *Washington Post*, "is bring them home."

way he died. "To some people, suicide does make a difference, unfortunately,"[98] said Ted Bowers, a chaplain and a veteran of the Persian Gulf War.

Some experts guessed that those who took their own lives had been troubled by a combination of harsh living conditions, disillusionment with the war, and being forced to serve longer deployments. Veterans advocacy groups were not happy with guesses. They called for an investigation, so that other soldiers could be saved. "I don't really care about the statistical significance of these numbers (compared with other wars), but I do care that the Department of Defense aggressively meets the needs of these soldiers,"[99] said Steve Robinson, executive director of the National Gulf War Resource Center.

Some families also questioned whether the military had done all it could to help those who were gone. Rebecca Suell, whose husband Joseph committed suicide in June 2003, stated, "They didn't take the time out to see if there was a problem with my husband. They don't take time out to see what these people are going through. These people [the soldiers] are concerned about staying alive—and they're stressed about their wife and children."[100]

Female Combatants

The news that a loved one had been taken as a POW was almost as devastating for families as learning of a death. Life seemed to stop while friends rallied for support, yellow ribbons were tied around trees to symbolize hopes for a safe return, and families watched television nonstop, listening for breaking news.

When the faces of captured soldiers, usually looking nervous, exhausted, and on guard, appeared on television, everyone analyzed them anxiously. They also asked themselves dozens of painful questions, such as "Had the soldiers been tortured?" "Were they being fed?" or "Had the women been sexually assaulted?" Claude Johnson, father of Specialist Shoshana Johnson, who had been captured in Iraq in March 2003, expressed his feelings. "We

Televised images of female POWs like Shoshana Johnson caused many Americans to question the appropriateness of placing women in combat.

know that she *was* alive [when they took the picture]. But is she alive now? And is somebody taking care of her injuries?"[101]

The fact that women were taken as prisoners of war in Iraq revived discussion among Americans about the appropriateness of placing women in combat situations where they could be captured. The issue had been debated before, but a law passed in 1994 had opened up most positions in the military to women.

There were at least two points of view. Many Americans believed that women had the right to serve in the military in the same way that men did. To place barriers in the way of their service was a form of sexism. Others believed that placing women in combat was unfair both to them and to their fellow male soldiers. They said that women were physically weaker than men and thus were less able to prevent their own capture. They were more vulnerable to abuse. Their capture was more likely to provoke public outcry. Their being present in a combat scene not only put them at greater risk, it potentially put greater responsibilities on their male comrades to protect them.

Retired U.S. Air Force lieutenant general Robert D. Springer saw both sides of the coin:

If women are to be permitted in all combat organizations on an equal footing, it should be for the right reasons. That is because they want to serve . . .

they are qualified . . . and they will enhance combat readiness. . . .

Is it necessary to place women in these combat roles? No. Would I want my daughters to serve in combat specific career fields? No. I realize my generation has a more conservative view on this issue than the younger generation. That may be because more of us have served in the military. More of us have seen combat up close and personal. Combat is not pretty, and it is not for everybody.[102]

Homecomings

Because the war in Iraq was so dangerous and deployments were so long, there was no happier day for military families than when their loved ones returned to the United States. Reunions were joyful. Soldiers hugged their families. Spouses and parents cried. Welcome-home parties were the order of the day. "I was running over people to get to him,"[103] remembered Sandi Rostan of Hot Springs, Arkansas, of when she was reunited with her husband at Fort Hood, Texas.

Some families and friends had even waited to celebrate Christmas or a birthday until the loved one's return. "We still have the tree up and the gifts are still under it," said Beverly Fox, a close friend of Specialist Stephanie Fought, who had been away for almost a year.

Homecomings were not always the joyous occasions that everyone expected, however. Old routines were sometimes hard to

A sailor returning from Iraq receives a joyful homecoming in San Diego.

resume. Husbands who had once handled responsibilities such as finances or outdoor chores found that wives had capably taken them on. Wives who expected help around the house from their newly returned husbands were disappointed when such did not happen. Fought noted that "getting used to being home will take awhile. I've been gone so long, it'll take awhile to get adjusted."[104]

Some returning veterans were angry and impatient with their families, a reaction to the stress and brutality they had lived through overseas. The result could be arguments, abuse, and sometimes divorce. Families were left bewildered and shaken. "I sent one person [overseas]. I got

66

make sure that I'm safe."[109] Retail sales of everything from appliances to automobiles plummeted. Businesses at tourist destinations such as Hawaii, the Grand Canyon, and Walt Disney World saw fewer visitors and endured heavy losses in revenue. There were also losses that few Americans ever noted. For instance, one media analyst determined that the Walt Disney Company lost $10 million per day from preempted advertising on ABC (which it owns) when that network broadcast news nonstop for more than three days.

Even when the initial shock of the attacks passed, the economy remained in a slump. Not even the war in Afghanistan brought about a significant boost. Businesses cut back on investment and spending, laid off employees, and initiated cost-cutting measures in order to survive. Families, fearful of everything from terror attacks to losing their jobs, made fewer purchases and tried to save more. The only healthy segment was the housing construction market; people continued to buy homes due to extremely low interest rates that made mortgages attractive. Financial commentator Mark Gongloff explained what a boost this was, both to the economy and to people's spirits: "When people buy houses, they often buy furniture, paint brushes, lawn mowers and an armada of other consumer goods to pretty up those houses. Even homeowners who haven't refinanced or bought a new house have enjoyed the 'wealth effect' of higher home values."[110]

Wait and See

Because the prognosis seemed gloomy in early 2003, the nation adopted a wait-and-see attitude. Investors held onto their money. Businesses put off expansion and hiring. Even new home sales slowed somewhat, and orders for goods and services dropped. Stephanie Harkness, head of a medical equipment parts firm in California, was one who felt frustration when her customers waited to place orders. "[In one case] they have the money in hand but have been saying they're not willing to make an investment until they know how the war is going to play out."[111]

The businesses that were hardest hit by the uncertain times were those that operated on tight budgets and had little savings to fall back on. Usually small, they ranged from gift shops to online businesses. When fewer customers coupled with too little money, they often could not stave off bankruptcy and went out of business.

One of the largest commercial segments to be significantly impacted by the troubled times was the airline industry. Families continued to scale back vacations, driving instead of flying. Businessmen turned to electronic communication instead of traveling to meet clientele face-to-face. "We've initiated a policy of essential travel only,"[112] said Peter Buchheit, director of travel for tool-making company Black & Decker.

As a result, between September 2001 and April 2003 the airlines had lost $18 billion and had had to raise ticket prices and lay off one hundred thousand em-

another one back,"[105] said Cindy Vining, who separated from her husband of seventeen years after he returned.

Aware of problems families faced when veterans returned from war, the military issued guidelines they felt would make the returns easier. Some of those guidelines included not having too much alcohol in the house, not having high expectations for romantic reunions, and not having long lists of chores for spouses to immediately take on. Some families appreciated the guidance, but others only found it irritating. "They micromanage our husbands' lives; why do they have to micromanage ours as well?"[106] asked Jennifer Veale, who was married to a Black Hawk helicopter pilot.

The problems of dealing with war-related trauma did not fall to all Americans, however. Only about 1 in 125 was a part of the military. And most who served could be expected to return home and take up their normal lives without a great deal of difficulty.

The challenge of coping with the war economy was something every American faced, however. From the cost of gasoline to the difficulty of finding a job, ordinary people were affected in many ways. "Everyone is afraid of layoffs and the states are all broke," said Sandra Bierwagen of Michigan, who was as jittery as the rest of the nation over how the war in Iraq would impact the economy. "Why would anyone go do anything when they see all this [trouble and uncertainty] coming?"[107]

☆ Chapter 5 ☆

The War Economy

The United States' enthusiasm for going to war in Iraq was dampened from the beginning by the economy, which was sluggish and showed few signs of revitalizing in 2002. Businesses struggled. The stock market was unsteady. Millions were looking for work, and consumer confidence was down. If the war was going to make things worse, they were less willing to become involved.

Experts reminded everyone that, traditionally, war encouraged economic growth. Businesses that produced war matériel such as tanks, helicopters, weapons, and ammunition would expand and flourish. Thousands could find work in these businesses, as well as in the military. There would be a greater need for food, clothing, and other necessities for the troops, and that would boost support industries as well.

Improvement was not a certainty as the war in Iraq began, however. Experts opined that if the war motivated a retaliatory terrorist strike by Iraq or al Qaeda, repeating the devastation of September 11, the country could perhaps sink into a recession. If the war became prolonged, expensive, and widely unpopular, that, too, could affect the economy negatively. Economist Diane Swonk said, "There is a bit of paralysis being created by the fear of war itself and once the sand settles, you know, in Iraq, we'll be in a better situation to sort of figure out where we are, where we can go from here."[108]

In a Slump

Part of the economic uncertainty stemmed from the fact that the start of the twenty-first century had not been a prosperous time in American history. The country's economy had been troubled by unemployment, declining productivity, and slow growth even before September 11, 2001. The attacks on the World Trade Center and the Pentagon were devastating blows. The stock market closed to avoid a panicked round of selling. When it reopened several days later, the Dow Jones Industrial Average—the world's oldest stock market indicator—dropped more than 660 points, the greatest point loss ever recorded.

The travel industry was hard-hit as well when all U.S. flights were grounded for two days. When flights resumed, volume was dramatically reduced as thousands of Americans opted to travel by car or put off trips until the times were safer. Mary James, a student in Hawaii, was one who ope[ ]stated her concern: "I'm scared to fly [ ]is, for fear of something malfunction[ ]and now I have a good reason not to f[ ]all! . . . I'm willing to sacrifice anythin[ ]

Terrorist attacks on the World Trade Center towers in 2001 had a devastating impact o[ ]already troubled U.S. economy.

Holding Back

In the spring of 2003, many Americans stayed home and watched the news, waiting to see whether or not the war would have disastrous consequences for them. Their inaction had a negative effect on businesses, as correspondent James M. Pethokoukis explains in his article "Stuck on Pause," published in *U.S. News & World Report* shortly after the war began.

> To corporate America, the prospect that Operation Iraqi Freedom could possibly stretch from spring into summer is taking on the feel of the Hundred Years' War. Businesses fret that as long as the conflict's outcome is in doubt, consumer and business spending will remain frozen.
>
> "This whole deal is very similar to the run-up to war in 1990, where people were in a holding pattern waiting for things to end," says Robert Dieckman, chief financial officer at Basco Manufacturing in Cincinnati, a small firm that makes shower doors. "Orders have been softer, and my only concern is that if this turns into a four-month war, consumers will continue to hold back. . . . "
>
> Then there's the "CNN effect," or, more appropriately these days, the Fox News effect. "Watching all this war coverage is preventing us from going to stores and showrooms," says [Carl] Tannenbaum, [chief economist at La Salle Bank in Chicago.] Indeed, J.D. Power and Associates data show that auto sales are down 8 percent since the start of the war. . . . For businesses that were already in a conservative mode . . . the prospect of a longer war probably doesn't change much: They were not spending madly or hiring in droves before the war started, and they sure won't be now.

ployees. Some, such as United and US Airways, had gone bankrupt or filed for Chapter 11, a prelude to bankruptcy. Cutbacks in flights, longer layovers, elimination of meals, and the like had made air travel a less convenient option for travelers. "The airlines have eliminated a lot of red-eyes through a lot of cities," said Major League Baseball umpire Hunter Wendelstedt, who had used those late night flights to get home to his family quickly. "Now, I often fly out of a city the next morning."[113] Many people estimated that fears over war in Iraq would result in 52 million fewer airline passengers, seventy thousand more layoffs in personnel, and a further reduction in flights.

Saddam and Oil

Another economic uncertainty that airlines and others faced in early 2003 was the cost and availability of oil, gasoline, and other types of fuel. The United States relied on Iraqi oil, and no one knew what Saddam would do with his country's oil fields if he were threatened. Some believed he might set them on fire, as he had done during the Persian Gulf War. This would not only cut off U.S. supply, it would create an environmental crisis with which American troops would have to cope.

Even if Saddam did not use oil as a weapon, Americans feared that other oil-rich Middle Eastern countries might. Iran, Iraq, Kuwait, Libya, Qatar, Saudi Arabia,

The Oil Factor

When U.S. foreign policy focuses on the Middle East, some Americans become convinced that a desire for oil is involved. As Adam Zagorin wrote in "All About the Oil," in *Time* magazine, control of the vital product was not the motivating factor for removing Saddam, but his overthrow had the potential to benefit American oil companies in the future.

Protesters chant, "No War for Oil." White House spokesman Ari Fleischer replied last week [February 2003], "if this had anything to do with oil, the position of the United States would be to lift the sanctions [imposed by the United States in 1990] so the oil could flow. This is not about that. This is about . . . protecting the American people."

The takeover and occupation of Iraq, perhaps for a decade or more, could cost American taxpayers up to $200 billion. Virtually none of that will be covered by the sale of Iraqi petroleum. At least that's what Secretary of State Colin Powell told the press recently. "The one thing I can assure you of is that the oil will be held in trust for the Iraqi people, to benefit the Iraqi people," Powell said. "This is a legal obligation that the occupying power will have."

A post-Saddam government in Baghdad could be expected to favor U.S. companies [however]. Ahmed Chalabi, a leader of the Iraqi National Congress, the most powerful exile group, has met with US oil executives and promised that American oil companies would benefit following a campaign to oust Saddam.

Protesters in New York condemn the war in Iraq as a ploy to secure control of oil interests in the region.

and the United Arab Emirates were all members of the Organization of the Petroleum Exporting Countries (OPEC). Formed in 1960, OPEC controls oil production and exports upon which the United States is dependent. If war sparked hostilities from them, raising oil prices would be a profitable way for them to express their anger. Those higher prices would translate into an increased cost of living for a variety of reasons. Heating oil and gasoline prices would rise. So would the price of all types of products as increased shipping and energy costs were passed along to consumers. "I think we [will see it] in higher food costs, higher transportation costs and vacation costs," said market analyst Phil Flynn. "We've seen some companies (report) that higher energy costs are going to be cutting their profits." [114]

There was little that anyone on the home front could do to avoid the problem. Ordinary Americans tried, however. In response to uncertainty about oil—including predictions that heating oil and gasoline prices were set to rise precipitously—some took steps to reduce their personal dependence on the products. Many joined carpools. Some cut back on the number of errands they ran, consolidating trips to the grocery store and using the bus instead of the family car.

Some of the most environmentally aware bought "hybrid" cars that ran on a

A projected oil shortage caused by the war drove some Americans to buy energy efficient "hybrid" cars like the Toyota Prius.

combination of gasoline and electricity. Getting forty-five to sixty-eight miles per gallon, they seemed a positive alternative to traditional gasoline-powered autos that got poorer mileage and also produced poisonous emissions. "The public that are buying cars and trucks want to see less dependency on foreign oil," said Ed LaRocque, a manager for Toyota North America, which began marketing its hybrid Prius in the United States in 2000. "The combination of [the] rising price of (US) domestic oil and more awareness of the environment is also helping push awareness of hybrids." [115]

"A Human Tragedy"

The tough economy with its uncertainties over the war not only translated into worries over oil, it translated into a tight job market. More than 2 million jobs had been lost in the United States since 2001. Some businesses had simply cut their number of employees in order to survive. Some realized that due to computers, some positions could be eliminated. Many offices no longer employed secretaries, for instance, since every worker had a personal computer, keyboarding skills, and could type their own letters and reports.

In some cases, employers turned to countries such as India and China, where costs were lower and workers were content with lower pay. Companies ranging from Nike, with shoes made in Indonesia, to Wal-Mart, with blue jeans from Bangladesh, had taken advantage of this cost-saving technique. Even businesses that were American legends, like Buck Knives, for example, had been forced to commission some of their goods overseas in order to remain competitive. Chuck Buck, the company's founder, explained, "We were getting pressure from dealers to lower our prices. Our filleting knives were selling for $26. Foreign knives were going for $14."[116] The outsourcing put a dozen Buck employees out of a job.

With fewer jobs available, everyone felt the pinch. Graduating college students had to look hard for first-time employment. Blue-collar workers with twenty or more years of experience competed for a diminishing number of manufacturing or service positions. Even professionals such as engineers and attorneys, who were normally more secure during economic downturns, became part of the unemployed job force.

Those who lost a job discovered that it took an average of five months before they found another. Most lived on unemployment until they could find something else to do, and sometimes ran out of benefits before they found work. Editor Matthew Rothschild wrote,

> Almost nine million people are unemployed today. Of those, two million have been unemployed for twenty-seven months or more—a depressingly high proportion. . . . 2.3 million more are not even included in the unemployment statistics because they are too discouraged to look for work. Every one of these eleven-million-plus individuals is a human tragedy.[117]

Making Compromises

Some of the most proactive job seekers attended training seminars where they could be retrained for new jobs. Angelo Cenotti, a job hunter in Connecticut explained. "You go online and look for certain job aspects and you get tools on how to better yourself, like preparing yourself for interviews and stuff like that."[118]

Job seekers also made compromises. They settled for temporary work, part-time positions, jobs that paid less than their previous work, or jobs that offered no health and pension benefits. This meant they had less security and money to live on, but even an inferior job was better than no job at all.

Many union employees in businesses across the country were not laid off, but they were asked to make sacrifices. Some took cuts in salaries and benefits in order to remain with a company that was struggling. An agent for the Allied Pilots Association, representing 13,500 American Airlines pilots, noted compromises they made in 2003. "After intensive, seven-day-a-week negotiations for the past month, on Saturday evening, March 29, the Allied Pilots Association presented American Airlines management with $660 million in contract concessions annually. These concessions are primarily concentrated in proposed work rule changes and across-the-board pay rate reductions."[119]

Although some like the Allied Pilots Association agreed to take pay cuts, other unions were more determined to hold firm to wages and benefits that they saw as essential to the well-being of their members' families. Health care benefits in particular were worth thousands of dollars to a family that was hit with medical problems. "Our priority is that they don't mess around with our medical coverage," said Earl Henry, a retiree of General Motors and a member of the United Auto Workers in Detroit, Michigan. "We don't want to lose what we already have."[120] In order to maintain current salaries and benefits, some workers agreed to work longer hours or add extra tasks to their job description for the same amount of pay.

Sticker Shock

With everyone's mind on jobs and tight personal budgets, any mention of the cost of the war made Americans nervous. Even if the conflict were short and successful,

Job seekers stand in line at an Illinois employment office. The economic downturn after September 11 caused a job shortage in the United States.

everyone knew that rebuilding and maintaining order in Iraq in the postwar months was likely to be expensive.

As of 2003, no one had said what the total might be, and critics were speculating that the Bush administration had not addressed the question adequately. Democratic senator Edward Kennedy expressed the feelings of many when he said, "We can at the outset afford whatever is necessary to defend our interests, and the American people expect this, but we ought to also consider the economic impact. That is a question that is not asked, considered or spelled out as much as it should [be]." [121]

News about the Iraqi economy, published shortly after the fall of Baghdad, sounded ominous. The country was in worse shape than experts had estimated. For instance, the main oil refinery in Bagh-

This high school in Kirkuk was just one of many schools that looters and vandals damaged during the war in Iraq.

dad relied on fifty-year-old boilers that were duct-taped together. A major textile plant was fitted with British machines that were forty years old. "It's difficult to exaggerate the chronic underinvestment in Iraq's infrastructure over the past 30-plus years," said one U.S. official. "We were all surprised with how neglected, brittle, and fragile the infrastructure was here."[122]

Not only had Saddam Hussein allowed many things to deteriorate, but schools, transportation, and telecommunications systems had been destroyed during weeks of war and looting. Power plants had been stripped of equipment and parts. Hospitals had been plundered of beds, medical equipment, and even electrical fittings. The cost to restore everything was going to higher than expected.

In September 2003 Bush announced that $87 billion would be needed to pay for labor, reconstruction, and keeping U.S. troops in the country for an extended period of time. The figure was stunning to Americans. Representative Zack Wamp of Tennessee expressed public sentiment: "We were all hit with sticker shock: $87 billion is a huge number"[123]

Pessimists were quick to point out that even that huge figure could inflate over time. Columnist Molly Ivins noted, "The eeriest part about Bush's $87 billion request is that it may not be enough. Sixty-six billion will go to the military and intelligence, leaving a relative pittance for actually rebuilding Iraq."[124]

Most Americans soon resigned themselves to the total, however. It sounded enormous, but they believed it to be reasonable, given the huge amount of work that needed to be done. The United States had spent billions rebuilding Japan and Germany after World War II. The nation was rich enough to foot the bill, and it had a vital stake in ensuring that Iraq became prosperous and stable.

By doing a little math, one man even put the $87 billion into perspective. He noted that, if that total was divided by the 290 million Americans who would be paying for it with their taxes, the total was only $300 apiece. Even twice that much was reasonable in his opinion, and he mocked budget critics: "I, for one, am absolutely *shocked* that the government might spend 600 dollars per American to topple a ruthless aggressive dictator, defend American interests in a truly 'progressive' Middle East, and liberate millions of people from Tyranny."[125]

Return of the Deficit

Americans understood the importance of rebuilding Iraq, but it was not easy to forget the cost, especially as the U.S. budget deficit (shortfall of money) seemed to grow larger with each passing day. Between 1998 and 2001, the government had actually taken in more money than it spent, accumulating a budget surplus of $127 billion as a result of growth in the economy and increased tax revenues. The economic downturn and September 11 attacks changed that. Because people were not spending as much, tax revenue (income from taxes) fell. At the same time, spending for homeland security and military operations rose, outdistancing income. As of September 2002, the government had used up the surplus and estimated it would spend $150 billion more than its income by the end of the year.

That was not the end of the story, however. Government spending continued, so that by early 2004, the Bush administration announced that the deficit would likely top half a trillion dollars that fiscal year. It would be the largest shortfall ever recorded in U.S. history.

A portion of the total stemmed from money needed to rebuild Iraq. Much was also a result of tax cuts made by the Bush administration between 2001 and 2003. Budget and tax expert Isaac Shapiro explains, "The tax cuts enacted in 2001 and 2002 will reduce revenues by $126 billion in 2003, based on CBO [Congressional Budget Office] estimates. The just-enacted tax cuts [in early 2003] will reduce revenues by another $49 billion this year."[126]

Most Americans were more disturbed by the notion of a half-trillion-dollar deficit than they were by the cost of the war. They knew the danger of overdrawing their own checking accounts and getting deeply into debt. They wanted the government to exercise the same wisdom and restraint in its financial dealings as they did. They also believed the cuts were ill timed. When everyone was willing to sacrifice to pay for the war, getting a tax refund seemed a move in the wrong direction. "I think they need to figure out how to pay for the war [first],"[127]

Hard Times

Working harder for less money was one of the economic realities Americans faced during the early days of the war. Jacki Harris of California was one worker who was hard hit. Journalist Daniel Kadlec tells her story in the *Time* magazine article "Where Did My Raise Go?"

Jacki Harris, . . . through no fault of her own makes 25% less than she did a few years ago. With overtime, Harris, 41, was making $59,000 a year for delivering airplane parts and keeping track of blueprints at a Boeing jet plant in Long Beach, California. She was relieved to keep her job through several rounds of layoffs. But as the ranks thinned, she lost her seniority edge and ended up as a clerk making $44,000 a year with no possibility of overtime. "I cried for a month," says Harris, a single parent with a 13-year-old son. "You do more with fewer people. They push and push." She is struggling with her mortgage, clipping grocery coupons and living in fear of losing her job. Says Harris: "I never miss a day of work."

said Joseph Ames, a twenty-eight-year-old cook from Boise, Idaho.

The administration insisted that the cuts were important because they would stimulate the economy. Businesses could use them to expand and employ more people who would thus have more money to spend. Tax revenues would increase, and eventually the deficit would be paid off.

Experts urged caution, however. A huge deficit, they pointed out, could cause a loss of confidence among investors. That could lead to a fall in the value of the dollar, a rise in interest rates, a decline in stock prices, and further reductions in household wealth.

"The scale of the nation's projected budgetary imbalances is now so large that the risk of severe adverse consequences must be taken very seriously, although it is impossible to predict when such consequences may occur,"[128] wrote former U.S. treasury secretary Robert Rubin and economists Peter Orszag and Allan Sinai.

Even supporters of the president such as Senator Olympia Snowe of Maine and Senator John McCain of Arizona argued that large tax cuts, even to those who needed them, were unwise when the budget deficit was growing. "I cannot in good conscience vote in favor of tax cuts, irrespective of their size or to which segment of the population they are targeted,"[129] said McCain.

Rebound

Despite the fears and anxiety, by mid-2004 Americans were surprised and relieved to see that the war had not produced the economic disruption many had predicted. The stock market had rallied on the good news that Saddam Hussein's regime had been overthrown without disruption to Iraq's oil fields or an attack on American soil. Gas and oil prices had gone up, but Americans were taking the hikes in stride. Consumer confidence had risen, as had spending and business activity. Federal Reserve chairman Alan Greenspan had stated in April 2003 that the economy was "prone to more long-term growth and not stagnation,"[130] which

most economic experts took as very good news. When Saddam was captured in December 2003, the stock market moved higher yet again.

By February 2004, jobs were being created and the nation's unemployment rate was gradually falling. Interest rates remained low, so housing construction continued. While most Americans feared the good times were temporary, they continued to trust in positive predictions, particularly those of Greenspan, whose expertise had

Federal Reserve Bank chairman Alan Greenspan reported that the U.S. economy was on the path to recovery after the Iraq War.

seen them through the hard times. He stated that month:

> The U.S. economy appears to have made the transition from a period of subpar growth to one of more vigorous expansion. . . . Productivity surged, prices remained stable, and financial conditions improved. . . . The most recent indicators suggest that the economy is off to a strong start in 2004, and prospects for sustaining the expansion in the period ahead are good. [131]

The good economic news was a blessing that every American welcomed. Nevertheless, not all were happy when they thought about the war, which was not going as well as expected. Progress in rebuilding Iraq seemed too slow. Violence was escalating. Iraqis seen on the evening news looked increasingly hostile toward U.S. troops. Some Americans were vocal in their impatience for the whole thing to be over.

No one had a definitive answer for how to bring that about, however. The result was debate, disagreement, and deadlock. International relations expert Robert O. Keohane understood the impasse, but believed that the country could not afford to let such a situation last for long. He stated:

> The Bush administration has recklessly blundered into the creation of a civil war, which we cannot easily solve and from which we cannot easily walk away. When asked how to solve the problem, it is tempting for those of us who opposed the war from the beginning to reply, "You can't get there from here." But we, as a people, are deeply entangled in Iraq, and we need to figure out how to respond. [132]

★ Chapter 6 ★

Division and Dissension

The war in Iraq continued to spark heated debate as the nation moved toward a presidential election in 2004. Much had been accomplished in Iraq. Saddam Hussein's regime had been toppled. The dictator had been captured, and a new government had stepped into power on June 28. More than one hundred thousand American troops continued to work to bring peace and order to the war-torn nation. Major Pete Wilhelm, with the Eighty-Second Airborne in Baghdad, described one of the ways his men were making a contribution in Iraqi neighborhoods and cities: "We set up a Neighborhood Advisory Council representative of each neighborhood, and they voted on a leader who attends the city advisory council. . . . We are making great strides at grass-roots democracy."[133]

The military accomplishments were tarnished, however, by the failure to find weapons of mass destruction, the high cost of the war, and growing anti-American sen-timent in the Middle East. Many Americans were convinced that the United States should have avoided the war at all costs. "We have to get the . . . troops out of there; they should never have gone to Iraq in the first place,"[134] said Sue Niederer, whose son was killed while trying to defuse a bomb in Iraq.

In the Streets

Niederer was one of fifty thousand demonstrators who marched in New York City to protest the war in March 2004. Many such protests and demonstrations had taken place since the war's beginning a year earlier. From Oregon to Florida, people had gathered in the streets, in libraries, and in private homes to share opinions and decide how best to make their messages clear. Matt Leber of Nashville, Tennessee, said, "We have been holding rallies and teach-ins that allow people to have their voices heard. . . . It's about raising public consciousness, asking questions."[135]

Most of the demonstrations had been smaller than those held during the Vietnam War era, when hundreds of thousands had turned out to protest government policies by destroying draft cards and burning images of the president. There had been some of significant size, however. The largest and most emotional took place at the beginning of the war when two hundred thousand protesters in San Francisco and New York City were joined by others in cities throughout the United States and around the world. Many marched, sang, and held up signs that said "War Is a Weapon of Mass Destruction" and "No Blood for Oil." Al-though most of the demonstrations were peaceful, in San Francisco demonstrators blocked traffic, smashed police car windows, and then dispersed throughout the city where they caused widespread disruption. "This is no ordinary day," said Jason Mark, an activist in that city. "America is different today: We've just launched an unprovoked, unjust war."[136]

Most of the protesters made it clear that they supported the troops and were

Demonstrators line the streets of San Francisco to block traffic as a sign of protest against the war in Iraq.

loyal to their country, even though they opposed the fighting. Many differed from Vietnam protesters in that they actually had loved ones serving in the military in Iraq. A few were Iraqi exiles who opposed a war in which their relatives and friends were being killed. "Maybe [my family in Iraq] survived the bombings, but are they going to survive the lawlessness?"[137] asked Rana Abdul-Aziz, a student at Tufts University who spoke at peace rallies.

The protesters were similar to earlier protesters in the various messages they tried to convey. In the beginning most tried to prevent the war, believing it was unnecessary and immoral. When that proved fruitless, other causes were addressed. Gordon Clark of the Iraq Pledge of Resistance was willing to use any and all grounds to thwart the war effort. He explained, "Some people want to try and achieve a troop pullout or push for the greatest amount of aid to Iraq. My dream is that this can be an ongoing campaign against the militaristic policies of the Bush Administration."[138]

Some protesters decided to make troop safety their emphasis. Others pointed out that the war was harming innocent Iraqis, too. They cited as evidence photographs that were released in May 2004 showing photos of U.S. military abuse against prisoners in Abu Ghraib prison in Baghdad. Professor Brian J. Foley observed, "The belief that America and American wars are God's gift to the world is naive. So is the belief that we can have a war without torture by both sides. . . . If we don't like the picture of ourselves from Abu Ghraib, then we should not like the war."[139]

Even Americans who supported the war were disturbed and saddened by the Abu Ghraib abuses. They had expected better of their troops and their government. Columnist Ellen Goodman wrote, "The scandals at Abu Ghraib do not slander every soldier, though they must dismay every soldier. But they leave an incredible imprint among those who love to hate us and hate to love us."[140]

The Debate over Loyalty

Counterdemonstrators who wanted their position to be heard joined those who protested the war. They, too, supported the troops, but they also supported the Bush administration and the U.S. mission in Iraq. They usually gathered in response to an antiwar protest and carried signs that read, "Support the U.S. or Keep Your Mouth Shut."

Some of the counterdemonstrators were simply passersby who reacted in anger to the protesters. Others turned out with a definite purpose. Alexis Zoberg, a student at Rutgers University in New Jersey, gave her reasons for speaking out in support of the government: "I'm a college student, so I'm exposed to a lot of liberal agendas, those within the classroom and the organized events on campus. I just figured someone has to put out the other message because it's not really getting put out there."[141]

Some Americans believed that criticizing the government during wartime was equal to treason. Criticism not only showed a lack of support for U.S. leadership, it undermined the confidence of the troops. If the enemy was listening, it encouraged him to believe that the United States was divided in its purpose. An editorial in the *New York Sun* said: "There is no reason to doubt that the 'anti-war' protesters—we prefer to call them protesters against freeing Iraq—are giving, at the very least, comfort to Saddam Hussein."[142] Those who supported this point of view displayed signs that read, "Saddam Sez, Thanks Suckers!"

Some, like televangelist Pat Robertson, argued that criticism of the war revealed an underlying hatred of America. "When people like Senator [Tom] Daschle [of South Dakota] stand up in the Senate and attack the president one day before the war starts, then that, to me, borders on lack of patriotism and I think it is wrong. . . . They hate America. It isn't just a war; they hate every-thing. They also hate the idea of standing up for freedom."[143]

While some Americans believed that it was wrong to challenge or question the government in time of war, others believed that dissent was not only acceptable, it was necessary. Allegiance to principles that the United States stood for, such as freedom of speech, political tolerance, and the rule of law, were as important as allegiance to a government. The advantage of living in a democracy was that people could discuss such principles, disagree with one another, reach a consensus—and in the end perhaps make the country a better place. Historian Howard Zinn, who encouraged critical thinking in the classes he taught, stated: "I want to prepare young people to say 'no' to the government. There are times where you might say 'yes' to the government, but I'm suggesting patriotism means being true and loyal—not to the gov-

"My Kind of Loyalty"

Throughout history, Americans have claimed the right to criticize the government, even in times of war. Mark Twain was one such man. In his novel *A Connecticut Yankee in King Arthur's Court* Twain explained his views on loyalty and the rights of citizens.

You see my kind of loyalty was loyalty to one's country, not to its institutions or its office-holders. The country is the real thing, the substantial thing, the eternal thing; it is the thing to watch over, and care for, and be loyal to; institutions are extraneous, they are its mere clothing, and clothing can wear out, become ragged, cease to be comfortable, cease to protect the body from winter, disease, and death. To be loyal to rags, to shout for rags, to worship rags, to die for rags—that is a loyalty of unreason, it is pure animal; it belongs to monarchy, was invented by monarchy; let monarchy keep it. I was from Connecticut, whose Constitution declares "that all political power is inherent in the people, and all free governments are founded on their authority and instituted for their benefit; and that they have AT ALL TIMES an undeniable and indefeasible [cannot be annulled] right to ALTER THEIR FORM OF GOVERNMENT in such a manner as they may think expedient."

Prowar supporters hold a rally in New York. Supporters and protesters of the war each questioned the other's loyalty to the United States.

ernment, but to the principles which underlie democracy." [144]

Top Level Dissenters

Some people at the top levels of government agreed with Zinn and felt that it was their right and their duty to question the

war. Often the dissenters were members of the Democratic Party who opposed the Bush administration on issues ranging from finances to the environment. Some, like former national security advisor Brent Scowcroft and former special envoy to the Middle East Anthony Zinni, were in the president's political party and were normally supporters of his policies. Their outspokenness was a measure of their conviction that the war was wrong, and it impressed Americans who harbored similar doubts but hesitated to express them.

Scowcroft opposed waging war in Iraq on the grounds that it detracted from the war on terrorism and could possibly lead to a wider war in the Middle East. He believed the United States was creating enemies around the world by going into Iraq. America's former allies viewed it as arrogant because it underrated their support. Its enemies saw it as anti-Islam when the war claimed Muslim lives. The resulting hostility hindered cooperation and progress in fighting al Qaeda and other worldwide terrorist organizations. Scowcroft said in August 2002, "An attack on Iraq at this time would seriously jeopardize, if not destroy, the global counterterrorist campaign we have undertaken." [145]

Zinni, a retired marine general, believed that many of the reasons for going to war—especially the arguments that Saddam Hussein was an imminent threat to the world

A National Responsibility

Senator Robert C. Byrd, one of the most senior members of the Senate, opposed the war in Iraq from the beginning. In an article, "Challenging 'Pre-emption,'" published in the online edition of the *Nation,* he encouraged Americans to speak out against what he considered President Bush's dangerous policies.

> As each day passes and as more American soldiers are killed and wounded in Iraq, I become ever more convinced that the war in Iraq was the wrong war at the wrong time in the wrong place for the wrong reasons. Contrary to the President's rosy predictions . . . the United States has not been universally greeted as a liberator in Iraq. The peace—if one can use the term "peace" to describe the chronic violence and instability that define Iraq today—the peace is far from being won.

> Iraqi citizens may be glad that Saddam Hussein is no longer in power, but they appear to be growing increasingly resentful that the United States continues to rule their country at the point of a gun. . . .

> A little more than a year ago, in October 2002, the Senate . . . handed to the President the constitutional authority to declare war. It failed to debate; it failed to question; it failed to live up to the standards established by the Framers [the nation's founding fathers]. . . .

> We must demand accountability from the Bush White House. We must continue to raise questions. We must continue to seek the truth. We must continue to speak out against wrongheaded policies and dangerous strategies.

with his weapons of mass destruction—were exaggerated. After visiting the region and studying intelligence, he concluded that the Persian Gulf War in 1991, air strikes against military infrastructure in 1998, and the imposition of sanctions and no-fly zones had effectively blunted Saddam's power. Zinni said, "He was contained. It was a pain in the ass, but he was contained. He had a deteriorated military. He wasn't a threat to the region."[146]

Zinni was also convinced that there were more dangerous scenarios than leaving Saddam in power: "I think a weakened, fragmented, chaotic Iraq, which could happen if this [war] isn't done carefully, is more dangerous in the long run than a contained Saddam is now,"[147] he said.

Members of Bush's administration, such as Vice President Dick Cheney, Secretary of Defense Donald Rumsfeld, and National Security Advisor Condoleezza Rice, did not side with Scowcroft and Zinni. From their intelligence sources, and from UN weapons inspectors who searched for weapons of mass destruction in Iraq up to the time of the war, they were convinced that Saddam Hussein had the potential and the inclination to inflict havoc on his neighbors and the world by the use of chemical, biological, and nuclear weapons.

Even those in government who were not part of the Bush administration shared that conviction. When a vote was taken in 2002 authorizing Bush to take military action against Saddam Hussein, most Republicans, almost half of all Democrats in Congress, and more than half of all Democrats in the Senate supported the motion. Senator Hillary Clinton of New York, one of the majority, noted:

> In the four years since the inspectors left, intelligence reports show that Saddam Hussein has worked to rebuild his chemical and biological weapons stock, his missile delivery capability, and his nuclear program. . . . If left unchecked, Saddam Hussein will continue to increase his capacity to wage biological and chemical warfare, and will keep trying to develop nuclear weapons. Should he succeed, . . . he could alter the political and security landscape of the Middle East, which as we know all too well affects American security. [148]

Missing Weapons

In 2002, most Americans were just as convinced as Clinton that Saddam Hussein possessed weapons of mass destruction. They had watched him obstruct the efforts of UN weapons inspectors in the 1990s and had heard those weapons inspectors speak in 1999 of his "practice of concealment of proscribed [forbidden] items, including weapons." [149] They had heard Secretary of State Colin Powell's compelling presentation to the United Nations in February 2003.

Thus, when UN inspector David Kay stated in January 2004 that the United States had been unable to discover any WMDs in Iraq after the fall of Saddam's regime, everyone was surprised and bewildered. They wondered how such a terrible mistake had been made. If Saddam had not possessed forbidden weapons, they asked themselves, why had he lied and evaded inspections, put his country through war, and ultimately caused his own downfall? If he had possessed WMDs, as intelligence sources had said, where had they gone? Senator Trent Lott asked, "We know he had biological and chemical weapons in the early 1990s. What happened to them? Did they move to another country? Were they destroyed?" [150]

No one could answer the questions about Saddam's line of reasoning, but there were several explanations for the mistake, and all of them had to do with U.S. intelligence shortcomings. First, intelligence sources had been unreliable. Many were Iraqis with ties to resistance leader Ahmad Chalabi, a former U.S. ally who hoped to assume power if Saddam was deposed. In May 2004, after a raid on Chalabi's home, investigators found proof that Chalabi had purposely directed his sources to spread inaccurate and misleading information in order to trigger a U.S.-led war against Saddam. To ensure that the information was accepted as truth, Chalabi had sent sources to several countries so that the information would be corroborated when it was shared.

Unaware that intelligence about WMDs was faulty, those who viewed and interpreted the hazy Iraqi surveillance photos and terse wiretapped conversations were biased in their point of view. They expected to see WMDs, and thus were satisfied that the photos depicted them. They also knew Saddam's reputation and did not want to minimize the threat he posed. Thus they fixed on the most ominous explanation of everything they saw and heard, and the resulting scenario they put together was flawed.

Many Americans were outraged by the mistake. They pointed out that the Bush administration had been too eager to be-

---

Ahmad Chalabi deliberately provided misleading intelligence in order to trigger a war against Saddam.

lieve in WMDs. It ought to have examined its sources more thoroughly, been more patient, and listened to those who were skeptical. They observed that, in light of the new information, the invasion of Iraq had been avoidable, irresponsible, and unjust. "Iraq, in retrospect, was no threat whatsoever to the United States. We fought an unnecessary war, and now we must rebuild a nation at a rising cost in blood and treasure,"[151] wrote conservative columnist Pat Buchanan.

Others, however, took a more philosophical attitude toward the administration's misjudgments. They deplored Chalabi's underhandedness, but accepted the fact that intelligence information was seldom perfect. Defectors and spies were sometimes deceitful and self-serving. And, they speculated, in the end, WMDs might still surface. Saddam might have moved them to another country or hidden them where they had not yet been found.

These Americans also argued that Saddam's overthrow was long overdue. The dictator should have been removed from power during the Persian Gulf War of 1991. He had been treating the United Nations with contempt ever since that time. He had defied their resolutions and even shot at U.S. fighter jets that were policing no-fly zones, protecting northern Kurds and southern Shiite Muslims from potential aerial attacks by Iraqi jets. Conservative commentator John Hawkins observed, "Worst case scenario, it's like we stopped a serial killer before he could kill again."[152]

Love Him or Hate Him

Just as the war in Iraq causes controversy, so does the leadership of President George W. Bush. John F. Dickerson and Karen Tumulty explain why in a *Time* magazine article, "The Love Him, Hate Him President."

Bush's approach to leadership has invited Americans to take sides. That's because he has resolutely swung for the fences in both domestic and foreign policy. Despite coming into office with nothing like a mandate [authorization by the electorate], he has governed as if he has one. As a result, Americans are divided over every big item on his ambitious agenda. Just as the country can't bring the war in Iraq to a tidy conclusion, it can't declare a truce over the fact that Bush took us there. For those who support him, the policy of pre-emptive engagement is the ultimate sign of his visionary grasp of what is needed

to fight and win the war on terror. "Something had to be done," said . . . . Bruce [Tenner of Des Moines, Iowa], who sounds a lot like Bush when he argues, "Over the long haul, if we can establish democracy in one nation over there, it's going to spread." . . .

For the increasing number who have doubts about the original mission to Iraq . . . Bush's policy was driven by everything from a thirst for oil to a crusading interventionist zeal. And the postwar problems bother them even more. . . . "I don't like the fact that Bush totally failed to finish the job in Afghanistan," says Bonnie Simrell of Westcliffe, Colorado. "I believe he withheld resources from that operation because he knew he wanted to march into Iraq. I didn't believe any of the arguments he made about going into Iraq. It was extreme folly."

Rebuilding Iraq

Those Americans who were outraged with U.S. intelligence shortcomings were also unhappy with the military's failure to quickly establish order in postwar Iraq. The initial overthrow of the government had been quick and easy, but efforts to rebuild had been challenging. Troops had been slow in restoring vital services. Insurgents had attacked and killed new Iraqi leaders and Iraqi police forces. The first U.S. occupation administrator, Jay Garner, was dismissed after one month over policy differences with the Bush administration. Iraqis who had rejoiced over Saddam's downfall had quickly turned on the occupying force, which they resented and wanted to see leave.

American efforts had been further hindered by hostilities that erupted between Shiite Muslims, Sunni Muslims, and Kurds, who were longtime enemies of each other. These three groups were formed into the nation of Iraq shortly after World War I by European conquerors who had ignored natural divisions when they went about nation building. Ethnic and religious hatred had continued ever since, but Saddam's repression had kept such feelings from boiling to the surface. Journalist Eric Alterman notes, "Iraq's reconstruction was always likely to be well beyond the capabilities of this Administration (or any administration), given the country's rampant factionalism, tribalism and various species of ideological radicalism."[153]

With such complications in mind, many Americans felt that the Bush administration had been negligent in not creating a realistic plan for rebuilding Iraq. It had failed to determine how newly unleashed ethnic hatred would complicate the process. It had misjudged the depth of anti-American feeling that existed among Iraqis. Former congressman Newt Gingrich, one of the critics, stated, "I am very proud of what (Operation Iraqi Freedom commander General) Tommy Franks did—up to the moment of deciding how to transfer power to the Iraqis. Then we go off a cliff."[154]

Again, not all Americans were critical. There were plenty who defended the progress that was being made in Iraq. They noted that little attention had been paid to the fact that among other achievements, most of the country's schools, hospitals, and banks had been reopened. Courts were functioning, and Iraqi ministers were running much of the government. Ordinary Iraqis tolerated and even appreciated the American presence: It was, in fact, terrorists and radicals, who saw the country as fertile ground for their operations, who were causing much of the divisiveness and the violence.

Supporters reminded everyone that rebuilding a country as large and complex as Iraq would be a long and difficult job. By working with those who were willing to compromise, and by providing the funds to rebuild, progress would continue. Columnist Mortimer Zuckerman wrote, "Iraq is just one place where the confrontation is direct, painful—and winnable.

. . . Many Americans, understandably, find the sacrifices we must make these days hard to bear, but they will support an effort that involves casualties if our strategy is clear and if they believe in its goals."[155]

Bringing in the United Nations

Among those who were critical of the rebuilding effort were those who believed that the United Nations should play a significant part in peacekeeping and reconstruction. However, Bush's decision to go to war in early 2003—with or without UN support—had alienated many allies who might have helped. General Wesley Clark observed: "The Administration went to the UN with a 'take it or leave it offer,' which reflected a combination of indifference and disdain. It did not explore every diplomatic option; it did not do everything possible to bring allies with us."[156]

No one could change the past, but as the rebuilding efforts hit snags, most Americans were convinced that an international body of UN peacekeepers could make the work easier and more effective. International troops would provide additional numbers on the ground, and would be less inflammatory than thousands of Americans who emphasized by their very presence that they were an occupying power.

The Bush administration responded by turning to the United Nations in late summer 2003 to request the formation of an international security force to fight growing insurgency problems in Iraq. Despite earlier opposition to the war, some UN members agreed to help with projects relating to humanitarian aid, reconstruction, refugee return, and economic development. U.S. deputy defense secretary Paul Wolfowitz stated,

We have no desire to own this problem or to control. Our only desire is what will get things fixed most rapidly. And you have to look at these pragmatically [prac-tically] case by case. More resources are great. Too many hands on the steering wheel, especially in the military area, is not great. But I think we've reached a very good understanding with the [UN] secretary-general [Kofi Annan].[157]

Iraqi leaders and a U.S. Army official take part in a school-opening ceremony in January 2004.

Pallbearers carry the coffin of UN special envoy Sergio Vieira de Mello, victim of a truck bombing in August 2003.

UN participation began in late May 2003. Workers were hindered, however, by the dangerous conditions that existed in Iraq, and top U.S. and UN representatives were targets of repeated attacks. After UN envoy Sergio Vieira de Mello, a respected diplomat with extensive experience in humanitarian and peacekeeping operations, was killed by a truck bomb on August 19, 2003, the United

Nations decided to pull out of Iraq. "I have always maintained that security was important for my staff to return," Annan stated. "Our activities are today constrained by the security environment. We need to have a secure environment to be able to go back and I'm not sure we have it yet."[158]

As of mid-2004 only UN ambassador Lakhdar Brahimi and his staff represented the organization inside Iraq. As special adviser to the secretary general, Brahimi had been asked to use his diplomatic skills to help choose new Iraqi leadership. Under his supervision, British-educated Iraqi neurosurgeon Ayad Allawi was selected as prime minister and began leading the country on June 28, 2004. No other UN representatives or security forces were expected to lend their aid in Iraq in the immediate future.

The 2004 Presidential Campaign

Diplomatic failings and divisions over the war were discussed heatedly as the presidential election of November 2004 drew closer. In the battle for the White House,

Americans asked the question, Who is the best man to keep us safe? The candidates' military backgrounds, their voting records on previous wars, and their plans for fighting terrorism became just as important as how they planned to strengthen the economy and improve education.

Senator John Kerry of Massachusetts became a front runner for the Democrats in early 2004. His qualifications to become commander in chief of a nation at war were impressive to some. He had demonstrated his patriotism by fighting in the Vietnam War, where he had earned three Purple Hearts for having been wounded in action. He had been educated at Yale and had

Senator John Kerry campaigns for the presidency in April 2004. Some Americans feel that Kerry would make a strong military leader.

served in the U.S. Senate since 1984, establishing a reputation as being strong on foreign policy.

Many Americans wondered if Kerry would be a strong and decisive leader when it came to war, however. After serving in Vietnam, he had returned home and spoken out against the conflict. He became a member of Vietnam Veterans Against the War, and even joined other protesters who discarded their medals onto the steps of the Capitol building in Washington, D.C. He had voted against going to war in 1991 despite the fact that Saddam had invaded Kuwait. And, as one Vietnam veteran noted, in recent times he had avoided taking a strong position when it came to Iraq: "Although Kerry voted to support military intervention in Iraq he is now claiming that he only approved the threat of force by the United States."[159]

Kerry's supporters contended that their candidate's record was better than his opponent's—President George W. Bush. As a member of the Air National Guard, Bush had avoided serving in the war in Vietnam. More importantly, his actions as president demonstrated that he lacked the ability to be a world leader. He had alienated the United Nations and other allies. He had stirred up anti-American feeling in the Middle East. He had gotten America deeply into debt with his spending for the war.

Bush's supporters disagreed with the critics and defended the president. They cited his outstanding leadership in rallying the nation to heal and rebuild after September 11. He had improved the nation's ability to protect its infrastructure, guard its borders, and patrol its skies. He had been decisive and diplomatic during the war in Afghanistan. He had been untiring in his efforts to advance the cause of justice, human dignity, and freedom throughout the world.

Those accomplishments seemed less impressive to critics in light of Iraq. Undoubtedly, the president had the courage of his convictions and was not swayed from the decisions he made, even in the face of strong criticism. But the war in Iraq had revealed a different side of him. He had come across as stubborn and unwilling to listen to those who counseled patience. Perhaps a different president would have been able to rally America's allies, bring greater order to the Middle East, and fight terror at the same time.

With homeland security and the war on terror as top priorities, Americans continued to debate the issues. Election day, November 2, 2004, would reveal what the final answer to their discussions would be. Keeping the war in mind, however, commentator Joe Klein believed that the results of the election would be based primarily on a single issue. "In the end, Bush and a Democrat will stand on the same stage," he said. "The central question will be a simple one: 'Have George W. Bush's policies made us safer in the world?'"[160]

A Cloudy Future

Homeland safety and security were the main reasons that Americans had supported going to war in Iraq in 2003. Yet more than a year after the opening attacks on Baghdad, they feared that their situation had become worse rather than better. The lives of hundreds of U.S. troops had been lost, and more seemed likely to be sacrificed in the struggle. A majority of the public felt convinced that growing hostility toward the United States in the Middle East made a terrorist attack on American soil more likely than ever before. Many experts shared that conviction. "The U.S. invasion of Iraq increased the worldwide threat of terrorism many times over,"[161] said author and terrorist authority Rohan Gunaratna.

Grim Possibilities

The reconstruction of Iraq itself bore the hallmarks of a situation that could spiral downward into failure. With the country a magnet for terrorists after the fall of Sad-dam Hussein, and with ethnic and religious divisions threatening to split the country, its future appeared extremely bleak. The transition government,which took control on June 28, 2004, faced enormous challenges. Newly liberated Iraqis were turning on one another in their push to have their political and social aims recognized. Government representatives from these groups had had trouble agreeing on a new constitution. No one felt able to predict that they would continue to compromise with each other in the future, or that they would be able to hold the country together in the face of divisiveness and postwar disorder. L. Paul Bremer, administrator of the U.S. Coalition Provisional Authority, stated in April 2004,

Iraq's democratic future is challenged by violent minorities. Groups old and new such as the Republican Guard, the Mukhabarat [Iraqi Intelligence Service], the Fedayeen Saddam [paramilitary founded by Saddam's son Uday],

The Impossible Dream

Although the Bush administration hopes to mold Iraq into a democracy, other Americans are less optimistic. Supporting their point of view is a CIA report, written before the war, that warned that the goal of democracy in Iraq was unattainable. Journalist Bryan Bender discusses the report in an article entitled "Iraq Democracy a Dream, Bush Told," found on the Web site The Age.

> The CIA's March [2003] report concluded that Iraq's society and history showed little evidence to support the creation of democratic institutions. It went so far as to say its prospects for democracy could be "impossible", according to intelligence officials who have seen it.
>
> The assessment was based on Iraq's history of repression and war; clan, tribal and religious conflict; and its lack of experience as a viable country before its arbitrary creation as a monarchy by British colonialists after World War I. The State Department came to the same conclusion.

Critics of the Administration's approach have said that pushing too hard to create a democracy could spark an anti-American backlash, increasing the risk of terrorism against the US.

"US efforts to impose a US vision on the area could lead to instability in countries like Jordan and Pakistan and could result in further strengthening the hand of fundamentalism and terrorism," Edward Walker, former assistant secretary of state for Near Eastern affairs in the Clinton administration, warned in a speech before the war.

and the so-called Mahdi Army [radical Shia militia] are trying to stop the process that leads to elections, to a government that respects the rights of all. They want to shoot their way to power. They must be dealt with.[162]

If conditions deteriorated too far, Americans would pay the price both at home and abroad. An Iraqi civil war was a real possibility. Shiite Muslims were already agitating for more power, sparking resentment from Sunnis. Clashes between the two groups could easily escalate into a general uprising and then outright war. Such conflict would destabilize the nation further, as well as possibly draw other countries such as Iran into the mix. In such an environment, terrorist groups would thrive, heightening the risk of attacks both on American soldiers in Iraq and on Americans in the homeland.

The Kurds could also set off civil war in Iraq. For years, most had wanted to declare an independent state in the north. They could take advantage of the political and social upheaval to try to achieve their ends. Their secession would not only create trouble in Iraq, it could inspire Turkey's Kurdish population to rebel. Turkey had opposed Kurdish autonomy for decades, so rebellion could again lead to a wider war. Journalist Bill Gertz wrote in 2002: "Turkish officials . . . warned the United States that Turkey regards parts of northern Iraq as Turkish territory. . . . [Their] message was meant to stress that Turkey will use force to stop any independent Kurdish state in northern Iraq and would not rule out annexing parts of the area."[163] Again, in such an unstable environment, terrorist groups could flourish and threaten the West.

In a third grim alternative, Muslim fundamentalists could gain control in Iraq and establish a government based on conservative Islamic law there. If that happened, repression could again become the norm. Religious freedom could be constrained. Women could be denied equal rights. Anti-American feeling would likely grow stronger. Again, the country could become an incubator for Islamic terrorism. If any of the above scenarios came to pass, in the words of one U.S. State Department official, "We are heading down a very dangerous path."[164]

A Brighter View

Despite the negative possibilities, many Americans were hopeful that good would come from the war. They acknowledged that there were many hurdles to overcome

Iraqi Kurds burn a Turkish flag to protest possible Turkish military intervention in northern Iraq.

and pitfalls to avoid before peace could be restored. Establishing democracy would not be easy because it was an unfamiliar concept in Iraq, and because the United States—the enemy—was sponsoring it. Senator Joe Lieberman of Connecticut noted in 2002:

> The Islamic world is beset by political, economic, and cultural circumstances that over the last generation have limited freedom and increased isolation, repression, and anti-American anger. These include vast income inequalities . . . economic and political isolation . . . and little or no democracy through which to constructively channel and resolve this strife. . . . We in America are its favorite target—not just because we are large and powerful, but because our cherished values of freedom, opportunity, tolerance, and democracy are its antithesis [exact opposite].[165]

With time and patience, however, many remained convinced that order could be restored, the country rebuilt, and friendly relations with Western nations be established. Most Iraqis seemed willing to do what was needed to achieve peace and prosperity. Despite the protests and acts of violence that made the news every day, they accepted the presence of U.S. forces because those forces checked the lawlessness and carried the promise of a brighter future.

Lieberman believed that the United States had much to lose if it did not continue to help bring about order and stability:

> If we don't help Islamic nations affirmatively choose the path of progress and peaceful coexistence by actively encouraging political reform, economic advancement, and cultural integration, the conditions that enabled yesterday's terrorists to kill 3,000 Americans will spawn many more and even worse threats to our nation and people in the future.[166]

"I Am Optimistic"

Although some Americans feared the outbreak of civil war in Iraq in 2004, U.S. Army general John Abizaid was more optimistic. His views are included in Marian Wilkinson's article "Top US General Raises Spectre of Civil War," published on the *Sydney Morning Herald* Web site.

> The Pentagon's most senior commander in Iraq, General John Abizaid, says it is "possible" Iraq could descend into civil war. Asked specifically whether Iraq could become embroiled in a civil war if attacks by terrorist figures such as Abu Musab al-Zarqawi and the group Ansar al-Islam continue, General Abizaid replied: "I believe that there is always the chance that through the wrong steps of political leaders inside Iraq and the deliberate steps of people like Zarqawi, groups like Ansar al-Islam and al-Qaeda are trying to move the country towards civil war, and that it is possible."

> But, he added quickly: "While I say it is possible, I do not believe it is probable. I think that there is a much greater chance that Iraq will emerge through this political process as a stable and modern state. . . . So, I am optimistic that we have a chance, but it is not a 100 per cent chance."

Whether democracy would one day be established in Iraq or not, Americans were resigned to the fact that for the time at least, they had to continue to have a presence in Iraq, both to maintain order and to offer guidance. The overthrow of Saddam gave ordinary Iraqis a chance to live in security and freedom. If those who wanted peace and prosperity could triumph over those who engaged in violence and repression, that freedom and security could be sustainable and might help change the character of the Middle East.

The alternative—a terrorist-ridden Iraq, free to express its hate for the United States at home and abroad—was unthinkable. As Alan P. Larson, U.S. undersecretary for economic, business, and agricultural affairs, stated in June 2003,

The long-term future of Iraq depends on the establishment of rule of law, representative government, and sustainable economic development. The United States, our coalition partners, the United Nations, and most importantly, the Iraqi people, must work together to finish the job, in order to guarantee peace and stability in the region, and safety for the American people. [167]

✫ Notes ✫

Introduction: War from a Homeland Perspective

1. Quoted in Fox News, "Iraqi Americans Celebrate Saddam's Capture," December 14, 2003. www.foxnews.com/story/0,2933,105712,00.html.
2. Quoted in Catherine Donaldson-Evans, "America Wakes Up to War," Fox News, March 20, 2003. www.foxnews.com/printer_friendly_story/0,3566,81701,00.html.
3. Melinda Liu, "Live from Baghdad," *Newsweek,* March 31, 2003, p. 33.
4. Quoted in Jim Axelrod, "On the Scene: In Saddam's Palace," CBS News, April 7, 2003. www.cbsnews.com/stories/2003/04/07/iraq/scene/main548185.shtml.
5. Quoted in Romesh Ratnesar and Michael Weisskopf, "Portrait of a Platoon," *Time,* December 29, 2003–January 5, 2004, p. 78.
6. Dennis Mountjoy, "Iraqi Freedom: A Gift from God," California State Assembly, April 14, 2003. http://republican.assembly.ca.gov/members/index.asp?Dist=59&Lang=1&Body=Opinion Editorials&RefID=535.
7. Quoted in Michelle Morgante, "Families of Troops Head to Baghdad on Peace Mission," *Peace Center News,* December 1, 2003. http://peacecalendar.org/archives/2003_12.html.
8. Quoted in Donaldson-Evans, "America Wakes Up to War."
9. Quoted in New Democrats Online, "No Divisions in the War on Terror," March 22, 2004. www.ndol.org/ndol_ci.cfm?kaid=131&subid=192&contentid=252467.
10. Nancy Gibbs, "The American Soldier," *Time,* December 29, 2003–January 5, 2004, p. 36.

Chapter 1: The Case for War

11. *Time,* "Overview: The U.S. Response," October 10, 2001. www.time.com/time/nation/article/0,8599,178464,00.html.
12. Richard N. Haas, "Wars of Choice," *Washington Post,* November 22, 2003, p. B07.
13. Quoted in U.S. Department of State, "Rumsfeld Praises Operation Iraqi Freedom Troops," March 20, 2003. http://usinfo.state.gov/topical/pol/terror/03032012.htm
14. Quoted in *Time,* "Overview: The US Response."
15. Quoted in The White House, "President Delivers State of the Union Ad-

dress," January 29, 2002. www.white
house.gov/news/releases/2002/01/
20020129-11.html.

16. Quoted in The White House, "Remarks by Samuel R. Berger, Assistant to
the President for National Security Affairs," February 13, 1998. http://clinton4
.nara.gov/WH/EOP/NSC/html/
speeches/19980213.html.

17. Quoted in The White House, "President's Remarks at the United Nations
General Assembly," September 12, 2002.
www.whitehouse.gov/news/releases/
2002/09/20020912-1.html.

18. Quoted in The White House, "President Bush Outlines Iraqi Threat," October 7, 2002. www.whitehouse.gov/
news/releases/2002/10/20021007-
8.html

19. Quoted in Kwame Holman, "Background: Talk of War," *Online News
Hour,* October 7, 2002. www.pbs.org/
newshour/bb/middle_east/july
-dec02/bkgdiraqpolls-10-07-02.html.

20. Quoted in Gleaves Whitney, "Democrats for Preemption," *National Review
Online,* February 13, 2003. www.national
review.com/comment/comment-
whitney021303.asp.

21. Quoted in Miles O'Brien, "General
Wesley Clark Analyzes Weapons Hunt
in Iraq," *CNN Saturday Morning News,*
January 18, 2003. www.cnn.com/TRAN
SCRIPTS/0301/18/smn.05.html.

22. "World Held Hostage," November 15,
1998. www.geocities.com/CapitolHill/
Congress/5747/WorldHeldHostage
.html.

23. Ciro Scotti, "Bush's Unfinished Business in Baghdad," *Business Week Online,*
January 11, 2002. www.businessweek
.com/bwdaily/dnflash/jan2002/nf200
20111_3437.htm.

24. Quoted in Karen Tumulty, "The Doubts
of War," *Time,* March 3, 2003, p. 43.

25. Paul Dellevigne, "Strange Days and
Manic Moments," Paulie the Suit, 2003.
http://home.earthlink.net/~ldellevigne/
paul_suit/manic.html.

26. Andrew Sullivan, "Yes, a War Would
Be Moral," *Time,* March 3, 2003, p. 44.

27. Quoted in Kelly Wallace, "James
Baker: Don't Go It Alone with Iraq,"
CNN, August 26, 2002. www.cnn.com/
2002/ALLPOLITICS/08/25/iraq
.baker/index.html.

28. Quoted in James Graff and Bruce Crumley, "'France Is Not a Pacifist Country,'"
Time, February 24, 2003, p. 32.

29. Prime Minister of Australia Web site,
"Transcript of the Prime Minister, the
Hon John Howard MP, Address to the
Nation," March 20, 2003. www.pm.gov
.au/news/speeches/speech79.html.

30. Quoted in James Graff, "The French Resistance," *Time,* February 24, 2003. www
.time.com/time/europe/magazine/
2003/0224/cover/story_2.html.

31. Rush Online, "Boycott France," March
31, 2003. www.rushonline.com/visitors/
france.htm.

32. Colin Powell, "Remarks to the United
Nations Security Council," U.S. Department of State, February 5, 2003.
www.state.gov/secretary/rm/2003/17
300.htm.

33. Quoted in *Online Newshour,* "UN Members Offer Mixed Response to Powell Report," February 5, 2003. www.pbs.org/newshour/updates/reac_02-05-03.html.

34. Quoted in *MidEastNews,* "Text of British Draft Resolution Presented to Security Council," February 24, 2003. www.mideastnews.com/UKdraft240203.html.

35. Quoted in The White House, "The President Says Saddam Hussein Must Leave Iraq Within 48 Hours," March 17, 2003. www.whitehouse.gov/news/releases/2003/03/20030317-7.html.

36. Quoted in Dan Eggen, "FBI Has War Plans to Mobilize Agents Against Terrorists," *Washington Post,* March 17, 2003, p. A01.

Chapter 2: "We're All Targets"

37. Quoted in John Hendren, "Saddam: A Man with Nothing to Lose," *Sydney Morning Herald,* July 8, 2002. www.smh.com.au/articles/2002/07/07/1025667088589.html.

38. Daniel Klaidman and Christopher Dickey, "Can Iraq Hit America?" *Newsweek,* March 17, 2003, p. 35.

39. Quoted in Klaidman and Dickey, "Can Iraq Hit America?" p. 32.

40. Quoted in ESPN, "Series Between Seattle, Oakland Canceled," March 18, 2003. http://msn.espn.go.com/mlb/news/2003/0318/1525822.html.

41. Quoted in Julie Scelfo, "We're All Targets," *Newsweek,* April 7, 2003, p. 10.

42. Quoted in Chitra Ragavan, "Insecurity Blues," *U.S. News & World Report,* March 10, 2003, p. 37.

43. Quoted in Eric Rich, "Guilty Plea in 'Test' of Air Safety," *Washington Post,* April 24, 2004, p. B01.

44. Quoted in Tracy Vedder, "New Technology to Defeat Terrorism in Our Ports," KOMO 4 News, March 15, 2004. www.komo1000news.com/news/story.asp?ID=30310.

45. Quoted in Vedder, "New Technology."

46. Quoted in Joe Klein, "How Soccer Moms Became Security Moms," *Time,* February 17, 2003, p. 23.

47. Quoted in Angie Cannon, "Taking Liberties," *U.S. News & World Report,* May 12, 2003, p. 46.

48. Quoted in Kris Axtman, "Interviews of US Iraqis: Outreach or Overreach?" Global Policy Forum, March 27, 2003. www.globalpolicy.org/wtc/liberties/2003/0327interviews.htm.

49. Quoted in Bill Mears, "Supreme Court Looks at 'Enemy Combatants,'" CNN, April 28, 2004. www.cnn.com/2004/LAW/04/27/detainees.

50. Quoted in Eils Lotozo, "Patriot Act Prompts Outcry by Librarians," Congressman Bernie Saunders Web site, April 19, 2003. http://bernie.house.gov/documents/articles/20030421102754.asp.

51. Quoted in Cannon, "Taking Liberties," p. 46.

52. Quoted in *Online Newshour,* "Liberty vs. Security," September 10, 2002. www.pbs.org/newshour/bb/terrorism/july-dec02/liberty_9-10.html.

53. Quoted in American Civil Liberties Union, "CAPPS II Data-Mining System Will Invade Privacy and Create Government Blacklist of Americans, ACLU Warns," February 22, 2003. www.aclu.org/Privacy/Privacy.cfm?ID=11956&c=130.

54. Quoted in Evan Thomas, "Al-Qaeda in America: The Enemy Within," *Newsweek*, June 23, 2003, p. 46.

55. Maxwell McCombs, "The Agenda-Setting Role of the Mass Media in the Shaping of Public Opinion," Suntory and Toyota International Centres for Economics and Related Disiplines, London School of Economics, 1997. http://sticerd.lse.ac.uk/dps/extra/McCombs.pdf.

Chapter 3: The War and the Media

56. Bill O'Reilly, "Media Must Stand Firm Against the Race Card," *New York Daily News*, March 3, 2003. www.nydailynews.com/news/ideas_opinions/story/63940p-59598c.html.

57. Quoted in Steven Plaut, "Best Examples of Media Bias for the Year, If It Won't Ruin Your Holiday," Chron-Watch, January 10, 2004. www.chronwatch.com/content/contentDisplay.asp?aid=5425&catcode=10.

58. Quoted in Chuck Wagner, "Study: Network Coverage Fair on Iraq War," *Pentagram*, September 26, 2003. www.dcmilitary.com/army/pentagram/8_38/national_news/25465-1.html.

59. Quoted in Media Research Center, "In Their Own Words: What Members of the Media Say About Liberal Bias," May 12, 1996. www.mediaresearch.org/biasbasics/welcome.asp#Admissions.

60. Quoted in *Hannity & Colmes*, "More Americans: Iraq Worth Going to War," December 15, 2003. www.foxnews.com/story/0,2933,105813,00.html.

61. Robert Jensen, "Embedded Reporters Viewpoint Misses Main Point of War," Znet, June 8, 2003. www.zmag.org/sustainers/content/2003-06/08jensen.cfm.

62. Quoted in Local 10.com, "Media/Journalism and the War Coverage," March 25, 2003. www.local10.com/news/2062681/detail.html.

63. Quoted in Jeff Johnson, "Democrats Say Establishment Media's Iraq Reporting Biased," Cybercast News Service, September 24, 2003. www.cnsnews.com/ViewPentagon.asp?Page=/Pentagon/archive/200309/PEN20030924a.html.

64. Quoted in Laura Cruz, "Families Worry About Missing," *Lansing State Journal*, March 24, 2003. www.lsj.com/news/local/030324_pows_5a.html.

65. Quoted in Ellen Turkenich, "Who Owns the Story: America's Televised Battle for Cultural Supremacy," *Online Journal of Education, Media, and Health*, New York University, 2003. www.nyu.edu/classes/keefer/joe/turkenich.html.

66. Quoted in Dave Moniz, "Some Veterans of Vietnam See Iraq Parallel," *USA Today*, November 7, 2003. www.usatoday.com/news/world/iraq/2003-11-06-vets-usat_x.htm.

67. Quoted in Moniz, "Some Veterans of Vietnam See Iraq Parallel."

68. Quoted in Merissa Marr, "Grisly Images Stoke Media Debate," News 24.com, March 24, 2003. www.news24.com/ News24/World/Iraq/0,,2-10-1460 _1337716,00.html.

69. Quoted in Dave Cuillier, "Balancing News Reporting with National Security in the Age of Terrorism," Association for Education in Journalism and Mass Communication, April 21, 2003. http:// list.msu.edu/cgi-bin/wa?A2=ind0309 d&L=aejmc&F=&S=&P=4258.

70. Quoted in Aaron Zitner, "Ridge Revises Advice: Buy Duct Tape but Wait for a Signal," *Detroit News,* February 15, 2003. www.detnews.com/2003/ politics/0302/16/politics-85682.htm.

71. Quoted in Constitutional Rights Foundation, "Press Freedom vs. Military Censorship," 2003. www.crf-usa.org/Iraq war_html/iraqwar_press.html.

72. Chip Reid, "Recalling Life as an Embedded Reporter," MSNBC, March 15, 2004. http://msnbc.msn.com/id/4400 708.

73. Quoted in Merissa Marr, "'Embeds' Offer Graphic but Limited War Close-ups," Reuters, March 25, 2003. http:// uktop100.reuters.com/latest/Army/top 10/20030325-IRAQ-TELEVISION.ASP.

74. Reid, "Recalling Life as an Embedded Reporter."

75. Quoted in Jerry Adler, Barbara Kantrowitz, and Geoffrey Cowley, "'I Had a Terrible Feeling,'" *Newsweek,* April 7, 2003, p. 53.

76. Quoted in Alexander Coolidge, "Home Front Still Struggle for Families," *Cincinnati Post,* April 22, 2003. www.cincy post.com/2003/04/22/milit042203.html.

Chapter 4: Heroes at Home

77. Patricia Erickson, "Honoring Military Families," Family First, 2004. www.family first.net/pressroom/veteransday2000 .asp.

78. Quoted in Rich Vosepka, "More Loneliness Ahead for Utah Guardsmen's Families," Colorado Army National Guard, September 9, 2003. www.coloradoguard .com/webpages/dma/familyfocus.htm #_TOC50971900.

79. Denise Gonsales, "I'm Afraid to Look, Afraid to Turn Away," *Newsweek,* March 31, 2003, p. 9.

80. Quoted in W.F. Keough, "Extended Iraq Tour for Reservists Hits Home Front Hard," Colorado Army National Guard, September 10, 2003. www .coloradoguard.com/webpages/dma/ familyfocus.htm#_TOC50971885.

81. Quoted in Simone Carr, "Wives of Servicemen Face Hurdle with Deployment," Good News, Etc., 2003. www.goodnews etc.com/033B-TS3.htm.

82. Quoted in Andrew Dys, "Area Soldiers, Families, React to News of Extended Stay," Colorado Army National Guard, September 10, 2003. www.colorado guard.com/webpages/dma/family focus.htm#_TOC50971888.

83. Quoted in Bart Jones, "Long Island Families Coping with Reservist Delays," Colorado Army National Guard, September 9, 2003. www.coloradoguard .com/webpages/dma/familyfocus .htm#_TOC50971902.

84. Quoted in Jim Stingl, "A Private Battle," *Milwaukee Journal Sentinel,* October 2,

2003. www.jsonline.com/news/metro/oct03/174439.asp.

85. Quoted in Jon Krawczynski, "Alabama Hit Hard by Tour Extensions in Iraq," Colorado Army National Guard, September 9, 2003. www.coloradoguard.com/webpages/dma/familyfocus.htm#_Alabama_hit_hard.

86. Quoted in Melanie Markley, "Deployment: Family Watches Soldier Go to War—Again," *Houston Chronicle*, March 26, 2003. www.chron.com/cs/CDA/ssistory.mpl/special/iraq/1836455.

87. Quoted in MSNBC, "Home Front: One Family's Struggle to Make Ends Meet," 2003. www.msnbc.com/local/KGET/M285909.asp.

88. Quoted in *Cincinnati Enquirer*, "Reservist's Business Dies in His Absence," January 5, 2004. www.enquirer.com/editions/2004/01/05/loc_loc1breserv.html.

89. Quoted in Krawczynski, "Alabama Hit Hard by Tour Extensions in Iraq."

90. Quoted in C. Benjamin Ford, "Duty, Business Mix for Employers," *Business Gazette*, April 30, 2004. www.gazette.net/200418/business/news/2148171html.

91. Quoted in PhillyBurbs.com, "House Passes Package of Bills to Aid Reservists, Emergency Crews," March 23, 2004. www.phillyburbs.com/pb-dyn/news/103-03232004-269875.html.

92. Quoted in Ryan Lenz, "Soldiers in Iraq Buy Their Own Body Armor," *Guardian Unlimited*, March 26, 2004.

www.guardian.co.uk/worldlatest/story/0,1280,-3904926,00.html.

93. Quoted in Al Jazeera, "Soldiers' Families Accuse US of Betrayal," October 2, 2003. http://english.aljazeera.net/NR/exeres/9D65692E-7033-41E2-B8E8-E3B4685C21EA.htm.

94. Quoted in Wes Allison, "In a Soldiers' Haven, Worry and Frustration Taking a Toll," *St. Petersburg Times*, November 7, 2003, p. 1A.

95. Quoted in Eileen Kelley, "Extensions of Duty in Iraq Stir Anger," Colorado Army National Guard, September 10, 2003. www.coloradoguard.com/webpages/dma/familyfocus.htm#_Extensions_of_duty.

96. Quoted in News Net 5.com, "Son Killed in Iraq 24 Hours After Talking to Ohio Family," April 12, 2004. www.newsnet5.com/news/2995054/detail.html.

97. Quoted in Brian Williams, "Helping Soldiers' Families Cope," MSNBC, February 2, 2004. www.msnbc.msn.com/id/4138080.

98. Quoted in Gregg Zoroya, "Soldier's Suicide Shocks PA Town," *USA Today*, October 12, 2003. www.usatoday.com/news/nation/2003-10-12-suicide-inside-usat_x.htm.

99. Quoted in Joe Garner, "Suicide Sparks Questions," *Rocky Mountain News*, March 18, 2004. www.rockymountainnews.com/drmn/state/article/0,1299,DRMN_21_2738761,00.html.

100. Quoted in Michael Martinez, "Army's Suicide Rate Has Outside Experts Alarmed," Common Dreams News

Center, December 30, 2003. www
.commondreams.org/headlines03/
1230-01.htm.

101. Quoted in Cathy Booth Thomas, "Taken by Surprise," *Time,* April 7, 2003, p. 65.

102. Robert D. Springer, "Women in Combat," WRAL.com, 2004. www.wral.com/fayettevillenews/890764/detail.html.

103. Quoted in ABC24.com. "Arkansas Soldiers Return from Iraq," April 2004. www.abc24.com/news/tristate/story .aspx?content_id=26322787826D-4602-A562-681877FEECFB.

104. Quoted in Adrian Burns, "Area Soldiers Return from Iraq," *Elyria (Ohio) Chronicle-Telegram,* January 26, 2004. www.chronicletelegram.com/Archive/Html/2004/January/1-26/Daily%20 Pages/Local/Html/local3.html.

105. Quoted in Colorado Army National Guard, "Soldiers' Return Can Cause Turmoil," 2003. www.coloradoguard. com/webpages/dma/familyfocus.htm #_Soldiers'_return_can.

106. Quoted in Jerry Adler, "Families Ask Why," *Newsweek,* August 4, 2003, p. 30.

107. Quoted in Nancy Gibbs, "A Nation on Edge," *Time,* February 24, 2003, p. 23.

Chapter 5: The War Economy

108. Quoted in *CNN Live at Daybreak,* "Hidden Costs of War," March 3, 2003. www.cnn.com/TRANSCRIPTS/0303/03/lad.14.html.

109. Quoted in Tracie L. Takatani, "MCC Students Speak Out," *Ho'oulu Online,* October 10, 2001. http://hooulu.org/10102001/speakout.html.

110. Mark Gongloff, "Housing to the Rescue, Again," CNN Money, January 22, 2003. http://money.cnn.com/2003/01/21/news/economy/housing/index.htm.

111. Quoted in Daniel Kadlec, "Why the Bear Will Lose Its Bite," *Time,* April 21, 2003, p. 60.

112. Quoted in Matthew Benjamin, "Bracing for Turbulence," *U.S. News & World Report,* April 7, 2003, p. 40.

113. Quoted in Martin J. Moylan, "Cutbacks a Headache for Fliers," Twin Cities.com, May, 23, 2003. www.twin cities.com/mld/pioneerpress/business/5924482.htm.

114. Quoted in Lorraine Mirabella and Bill Atkinson, "Rising Oil Prices Threaten Economy, Experts Warn," *Baltimore Sun,* May 7, 2004. www.baltimoresun .com/business/bal-te.bz.oil07may07,0,5 533727.story?coll=bal-home-headlines.

115. Quoted in Paul Eng, "Making Way for the Hybrids," ABC News, October 1, 2003. http://abcnews.go.com/sections/SciTech/Business/hybridcars031001-1 .html.

116. Quoted in Daniel Kadlec, "Where Did My Raise Go?" *Time,* May 26, 2003, p. 49.

117. Matthew Rothschild, "Bush's War Economy," *Progressive,* December 2003. www. progressive.org/dec03/com1203.html.

118. Quoted in Matt Scott, "Unemployment Up: Job Fairs Help Those Looking for Work," WTNH.com, March 7, 2003. www.wtnh.com./Global/story .asp?S=1169165.

119. Quoted in *Business Wire,* "Allied Pilots Association Presents $660 Million in Yearly Savings to American Airlines

Management; 'Meets Cost Savings Target Management Established at Onset of Talks,'" March 30, 2003. www.find articles.com/cf_dls/m0EIN/2003_ March_30/99462514/pl/article.jhtml.

120. Quoted in Mike Hudson, "Economy to Rule Auto Labor Talks," *Detroit News,* July 14, 2003. www.detnews.com/ 2003/specialreport/0309/08/a01 -216641.htm.

121. Quoted in *Boston Business Journal,* "Kennedy: Iraqi War Could Hurt US Economy," September 23, 2002. www .bizjournals.com/boston/stories/ 2002/09/23/daily9.html.

122. Quoted in Wayne Washington, "Bush Aides Admit Iraq Missteps," *Boston Globe,* September 9, 2003. www.boston .com/news/nation/washington/ articles/2003/09/09/bush_aides_admit _iraq_missteps.

123. Quoted in Yahoo! News, "Analysts Warned of Iraq War's High Cost," November 1, 2003. http://asia.news.yahoo .com/031101/ap/d7uhm2sg0.html.

124. Molly Ivins, "The $87 Billion Question," *Texas Observer,* September 26, 2003. www.texasobserver.org/showArticle .asp?ArticleID=1464.

125. Dean Esmay, "Discuss This Article," Dean's World, September 29, 2003. www.deanesmay.com/archives/005003 .html.

126. Isaac Shapiro, "Bush Tax Cuts to Send Revenues, as a Share of GDP, to Lowest Level Since 1959," Center on Budget and Policy Priorities, June 4, 2003. www.cbpp.org/6-4-03tax.htm.

127. Quoted in *St. Petersburg Times,* "6 in 10 Oppose Wartime Tax Cuts," April 14, 2003. www.sptimes.com/2003/04/14/ Worldandnation/6_in_10_oppose_ wartime.shtml.

128. Quoted in Nick Beams, "US Budget Deficit to Hit Half a Trillion Dollars," World Socialist Web Site, February 4, 2004. www.wsws.org/articles/2004/ feb2004/defi-f04.shtml.

129. Quoted in Mike Sunnucks, "McCain Opposes Tax Cuts," *Business Journal,* March 18, 2003. http://phoenix.biz journal.com/phoenix/stories/2003/ 03/17/daily29.html.

130. Quoted in Kadlec, "Why the Bear Will Lose Its Bite," p. 61.

131. Quoted in Federal Reserve Board, "Testimony of Chairman Alan Greenspan," February 25, 2004. www.federalreserve .gov/boarddocs/testimony/2004/ 20040225/default.htm.

132. Robert O. Keohane, "Avoiding the Worst in Iraq," *Raleigh News & Observer,* April 11, 2004. http://newsobserver .com/editorials/story/3504218p-31 08870c.html.

Chapter 6: Division and Dissension

133. Quoted in Karl Zinsmeister, "Progress Exceeds Prognostication in Iraq," *Christian Science Monitor,* October 20, 2003. www.christiansciencemonitor .com/2003/1020/p09s01-coop.html.

134. Quoted in ABC News Online, "Thousands March in New York on Iraq War Anniversary," March 21, 2004. www.abc .net.au/news/newsitems/s1070292.htm.

135. Quoted in *Nation,* "Antiwar America," March 12, 2003. www.thenation.com/doc.mhtml?i=20030331&s=antiwar.

136. Quoted in CNN, "Protests Swell in Wake of War," March 21, 2003. www.cnn.com/2003/US/03/20/sprj.irq.war.protests.ap.

137. Quoted in Louise Kennedy, "Demonstrators Say Peace Movement Will Continue," *Globe,* April 10, 2003. www.mfso.org/Globe1.html.

138. Quoted in Josh Tyrangiel, "Voices of Outrage," *Time,* March 31, 2003, p. 63.

139. Brian J. Foley, "Why the Outrage About Abu Ghraib?" *Counterpunch,* May 15–16, 2004. www.counterpunch.org/foley05152004.html.

140. Ellen Goodman, "The Ugly Americans," *Washington Post,* May 4, 2003. www.postwritersgroup.com/archives/good0503.htm.

141. Quoted in Chris Jolma, "Protest Warriors New Movement," *Washington Times,* November 18, 2003. www.washtimes.com/culture/20031117-092208-4242r.htm.

142. Quoted in Timothy A. Noah, "Dissent Equals Treason," *Slate,* February 11, 2003. http://slate.msn.com/id/2078455.

143. Quoted in People For the American Way, "Talking Out of Turn: The Right's Campaign Against Dissent," April 29, 2003. www.pfaw.org/pfaw/general/default.aspx?oid=10389.

144. Quoted in NPR, "Citizen Student: Teaching Patriotism in Time of War," February 7, 2003. www.npr.org/display_pages/features/feature_957688.html.

145. Quoted in Julian Borger, "US Adviser Warns of Armageddon," *Guardian Unlimited,* August 16, 2002. www.guardian.co.uk/Iraq/Story/0,2763,775532,00.html.

146. Quoted in Thomas E. Ricks, "Four-Star Marine General: Iraq Strategy 'Screwed-Up,'" Truthout, December 23, 2003. www.truthout.org/docs_03/122403B.shtml

147. Quoted in Ricks, "Four-Star Marine General."

148. Quoted in John Hawkins, "What About the Weapons of Mass Destruction?" *Right Wing News,* 2004. www.rightwingnews.com/john/wmd.php.

149. Quoted in 10 Downing Street, "Part 2: History of Weapons Inspections," May 19, 2004. www.number-10.gov.uk/output/Page277.asp.

150. Quoted in CBS News, "Kay: We Were Almost All Wrong," January 28, 2004. www.cbsnews.com/stories/2004/01/29/iraq/main596595.shtml.

151. Patrick J. Buchanan, "An Unnecessary War," *World Net Daily,* June 4, 2003. www.worldnetdaily.com/news/article.asp?ARTICLE_ID=32894.

152. Hawkins, "What About the Weapons of Mass Destruction?"

153. Eric Alterman, "'Sorry' Seems to Be the Hardest Word," *Nation,* January 29, 2004. www.thenation.com/doc.mhtml?i=20040216&s=alterman.

154. Quoted in John Barry and Evan Thomas, "Dissent in the Bunker," *Newsweek,* December 15, 2003, p. 36.

155. Mortimer Zuckerman, "The Case for Burden Bearing," Congressman Mark Kennedy Web Site, November 3, 2003. http://markkennedy.house.gov/cgi_data/reading/files/7.shtml.

156. Wesley Clark, "Clark Outlines Success Strategy in Iraq," Council on Foreign

Relations, November 6, 2003. www.cfr
.org/campaign2004/pub6533/wesley_
clark/clark_outlines_success_strategy_
in_iraq.php.

157. Quoted in Kwame Holman, "Iraq Challenge," *Online Newshour,* September 9, 2003. www.pbs.org/newshour/bb/middle_east/july-dec03/iraq_09-09.html.

158. Quoted in Thalif Deen, "Violence Stymies UN Efforts to Return to Iraq," AntiWar.com, February 13, 2004. www.antiwar.com/ips/deen.php?articleid=1968.

159. Ted Sampley, "US Veteran Dispatch," Vietnam Veterans Against John Kerry, 2004. www.usvetdsp.com/jf_kerry.htm.

160. Joe Klein, "The Question All the Candidates Must Face," *Time,* January 26, 2004, p. 29.

Epilogue: A Cloudy Future

161. Quoted in Ken Delanian, "Terrorists 'Creating Widespread Fear,'" *Biloxi (MS) Sun Herald,* May 9, 2004. www.sunherald.com/mld/thesunherald/news/world/8623945.htm.

162. Quoted in U.S. Department of State, "Violent Minorities Will Not Thwart Iraq's Future, Bremer Says," April 18, 2004. http://usinfo.state.gov/mena/Archive/2004/Apr/18-871777.html.

163. Bill Gertz, "Turkey Warns It Might Annex Northern Iraq," *World Net Daily,* August 28, 2002. www.worldnetdaily.com/news/printer-friendly.asp?ARTICLE_ID=28760.

164. Quoted in Joel Mowbray, "Iraq: Becoming an Islamic Republic?" Townhall.com, October 17, 2003. www.townhall.com/columnists/joelmowbray/printjm20031017.shtml.

165. Joseph Lieberman, "Winning the Wider War Against Terrorism," New Democrats Online, January 14, 2002. www.ndol.org/ndol_ci.cfm?contentid=250015&kaid=106&subid=122.

166. Lieberman, "Winning the Wider War."

167. Alan P. Larson, "Future of Iraq," U.S. Department of State, June 4, 2003. www.state.gov/e/rls/rm/2003/21267.htm.

☆ For Further Reading ☆

Books

Fred Bratman, *War in the Persian Gulf.* Brookfield, CT: Millbrook Press, 1991. An overview of the Persian Gulf War (1991), which set the stage for the Iraq War of 2003.

John Hamilton, *Real-Time Reporting.* Edina, MN: ABDO & Daughters, 2004. Offers a description of the concept of "embedded" journalists and gives a concise history of the press in earlier American conflicts. An easy read and a good overview of the topic.

Jason Richie, *Iraq and the Fall of Saddam Hussein.* Minneapolis, MN: Oliver Press, 2003. Includes the history of Saddam Hussein's rise to power, his years of rule over the Iraqi people, and the American invasion that ended his regime.

Gail B. Stewart, *The War at Home.* San Diego, CA: Lucent Books, 2004. Focuses on air travel, bioterrorism, the nation's borders, and other pertinent topics immediately after the terrorist attacks of September 11, 2001.

John F. Wukovits, *George W. Bush.* San Diego, CA: Lucent Books, 2000. Traces Bush's life, including his childhood, education, military involvement, personal life, business and outside interests, and campaign for the 2000 Republican presidential nomination.

Web Sites

Family and Friends of the 129th Transportation Company (www.129supporting oursoldiers.com). The site provides information and links between the military, military families, and citizens to find positive solutions to problems faced by reserve soldiers and their families.

Fisher House (http://fisherhouse.org). The Fisher House program is a private-public partnership that supports America's military in their time of need. The site provides information about how to get aid as well as the organization's scholarship and community service awards programs.

U.S. Department of Homeland Security (www.dhs.gov/dhspublic). Provides information on homeland security issues ranging from emergencies and disasters, threats and protection, immigration and borders, and research and technology. Includes information on the threat level, creating emergency kits, and making emergency plans.

✫ Works Consulted ✫

Periodicals

Jerry Adler, "Families Ask Why," *Newsweek*, August 4, 2003.

Jerry Adler, Barbara Kantrowitz, and Geoffrey Cowley, "'I Had a Terrible Feeling,'" *Newsweek*, April 7, 2003.

Fouad Ajami, "A Chronicle of War Foretold," *U.S. News & World Report*, March 31, 2003.

Wes Allison, "In a Soldiers' Haven, Worry and Frustration Taking a Toll," *St. Petersburg Times*, November 7, 2003.

John Barry and Evan Thomas, "Dissent in the Bunker," *Newsweek*, December 15, 2003.

Matthew Benjamin, "Bracing for Turbulence," *U.S. News & World Report*, April 7, 2003.

Angie Cannon, "Taking Liberties," *U.S. News & World Report*, May 12, 2003.

John F. Dickerson and Karen Tumulty, "The Love Him, Hate Him President," *Time*, December 1, 2003.

Dan Eggen, "FBI Has War Plans to Mobilize Agents Against Terrorists," *Washington Post*, March 17, 2003.

Daren Fonda and Sally B. Donnelly, "Bumps in the Sky," *Time*, November 3, 2003.

Nancy Gibbs, "The American Soldier," *Time*, December 29, 2003–January 5, 2004.

———, "A Nation on Edge," *Time*, February 24, 2003.

Denise Gonsales, "I'm Afraid to Look, Afraid to Turn Away," *Newsweek*, March 31, 2003.

James Graff and Bruce Crumley, "'France Is Not a Pacifist Country,'" *Time*, February 24, 2003.

Richard N. Haas, "Wars of Choice," *Washington Post*, November 22, 2003.

Daniel Kadlec, "Where Did My Raise Go?" *Time*, May 26, 2003.

———, "Why the Bear Will Lose Its Bite," *Time*, April 21, 2003.

Daniel Klaidman and Christopher Dickey, "Can Iraq Hit America?" *Newsweek*, March 17, 2003.

Joe Klein, "How Soccer Moms Became Security Moms," *Time*, February 17, 2003.

———, "The Question All the Candidates Must Face," *Time*, January 26, 2004.

Melinda Liu, "Live from Baghdad," *Time*, March 31, 2003.

Newsweek, "A Tyrant Captured," January 12, 2004.

James M. Pethokoukis, "Stuck on Pause," *U.S. News & World Report*, April 7, 2003.

James Poniewozik, "What You See vs. What They See," *Time*, April 7, 2003.

Chitra Ragavan, "Insecurity Blues," *U.S. News & World Report*, March 10, 2003.

Romesh Ratnesar and Michael Weisskopf, "Portrait of a Platoon," *Time*, December 29, 2003–January 5, 2004.

Hugh Rawson, "The Road to Freedom Fries," *American Heritage*, June/July 2003.

Eric Rich, "Guilty Plea in 'Test' of Air Safety," *Washington Post,* April 24, 2004.

Julie Scelfo, "We're All Targets," *Newsweek,* April 7, 2003.

Andrew Sullivan, "Yes, a War Would Be Moral," *Time,* March 3, 2003.

Curtis Taylor, "Letters," *Time,* March 17, 2003.

Cathy Booth Thomas, "Taken by Surprise," *Time,* April 7, 2003.

Evan Thomas, "Al-Qaeda in America: The Enemy Within," *Newsweek,* June 23, 2003.

Karen Tumulty, "The Doubts of War," *Time,* March 3, 2003.

Josh Tyrangiel, "Voices of Outrage," *Time,* March 31, 2003.

Adam Zagorin, "All About the Oil," *Time,* February 17, 2003.

Internet Sources

ABC News Online, "Thousands March in New York on Iraq War Anniversary," March 21, 2004. www.abc.net.au/news/newsitems/s1070292.htm.

ABC24.com, "Arkansas Soldiers Return from Iraq," April 2004. www.abc24.com/news/tristate/story.aspx?content_id=26322787-826D-4602-A562-681877FEECFB.

Eric Alterman, "'Sorry' Seems to Be the Hardest Word," *Nation,* January 29, 2004. www.thenation.com/doc.mhtml?i=20040216&s=alterman.

American Civil Liberties Union, "CAPPS II Data-Mining System Will Invade Privacy and Create Government Blacklist of Americans, ACLU Warns," February 22, 2003. www.aclu.org/Privacy/Privacy.cfm?ID=11956&c=130.

Jim Axelrod, "On the Scene: In Saddam's Palace," CBS News, April 7, 2003. www.cbsnews.com/stories/2003/04/07/iraq/scene/main548185.shtml.

Kris Axtman, "Interviews of US Iraqis: Outreach or Overreach?" Global Policy Forum, March 27, 2003. www.globalpolicy.org/wtc/liberties/2003/0327interviews.htm.

Nick Beams, "US Budget Deficit to Hit Half a Trillion Dollars," World Socialist Web Site, February 4, 2004. www.wsws.org/articles/2004/feb2004/defi-f04.shtml.

Bryan Bender, "Iraq Democracy a Dream, Bush Told," The Age, August 15, 2003. www.theage.com.au/articles/2003/08/14/1060588524354.html.

Julian Borger, "US Adviser Warns of Armageddon," *Guardian Unlimited,* August 16, 2002. www.guardian.co.uk/Iraq/Story/0,2763,775532,00.html.

Boston Business Journal, "Kennedy: Iraqi War Could Hurt US Economy," September 23, 2002. www.bizjournals.com/boston/stories/2002/09/23/daily9.html.

Patrick J. Buchanan, "An Unnecessary War," *World Net Daily,* June 4, 2003. www.worldnetdaily.com/news/article.asp?ARTICLE_ID=32894.

Adrian Burns, "Area Soldiers Return from Iraq," *Elyria (Ohio) Chronicle-Telegram,* January 26, 2004. www.chronicletelegram.com/Archive/Html/2004/January/1-26/Daily%20Pages/Local/Html/local3.html.

Business Wire, "Allied Pilots Association Presents $660 Million in Yearly Savings to American Airlines Management; 'Meets Cost Savings Target Management Established at Onset of Talks,'" March 30,

2003. www.findarticles.com/cf_dls/m0 EIN/2003_March_30/99462514/pl/article.jhtml.

Robert C. Byrd, "Challenging 'Pre-emption,'" *Nation,* December 14, 2003. www.thenation.com/doc.mhtml?i=20031229&s=byrd.

Simone Carr, "Wives of Servicemen Face Hurdle with Deployment," Good News, Etc., 2003. www.goodnewsetc.com/033B-TS3.htm.

CBS News, "Kay: We Were Almost All Wrong," January 28, 2004. www.cbsnews.com/stories/2004/01/29/iraq/main596595.shtml.

Cincinnati Enquirer, "Reservist's Business Dies in His Absence," January 5, 2004. www.enquirer.com/editions/2004/01/05/loc_loc1breserv.html.

Wesley Clark, "Clark Outlines Success Strategy in Iraq," Council on Foreign Relations, November 6, 2003. www.cfr.org/campaign2004/pub6533/wesley_clark/clark_outlines_success_strategy_in_iraq.php.

CNN, "Protests Swell in Wake of War," March 21, 2003. www.cnn.com/2003/US/03/20/sprj.irq.war.protests.ap.

CNN Live at Daybreak, "Hidden Costs of War," March 3, 2003. www.cnn.com/TRANSCRIPTS/0303/03/lad.14.html.

Colorado Army National Guard, "Soldiers' Return Can Cause Turmoil," 2003. www.coloradoguard.com/webpages/dma/familyfocus.htm#_Soldiers'_return_can.

Constitutional Rights Foundation, "Press Freedom vs. Military Censorship," 2003. www.crf-usa.org/Iraqwar_html/iraqwar_press.html.

Alexander Coolidge, "Home Front Still Struggle for Families," *Cincinnati Post,* April 22, 2003. www.cincypost.com/2003/04/22/milit042203.html.

Laura Cruz, "Families Worry About Missing," *Lansing State Journal,* March 24, 2003. www.lsj.com/news/local/030324_pows_5a.html.

Dave Cuillier, "Balancing News Reporting with National Security in the Age of Terrorism," Association for Education in Journalism and Mass Communication, April 21, 2003. http://list.msu.edu/cgi-bin/wa?A2=ind0309d&L=acjmc&F=&S=&P=4258.

Thalif Deen, "Violence Stymies UN Efforts to Return to Iraq," AntiWar.com, February 13, 2004. www.antiwar.com/ips/deen.php?articleid=1968.

Ken Delanian, "Terrorists 'Creating Widespread Fear,'" *Biloxi (MS) Sun Herald,* May 9, 2004. www.sunherald.com/mld/thesunherald/news/world/8623945.htm.

Paul Dellevigne, "Strange Days and Manic Moments," Paulie the Suit, 2003. http://home.earthlink.net/~ldellevigne/paul_suit/manic.html.

Catherine Donaldson-Evans, "America Wakes Up to War," Fox News, March 20, 2003. www.foxnews.com/printer_friendly_story/0,3566,81701,00.html.

Andrew Dys, "Area Soldiers, Families, React to News of Extended Stay," Colorado Army National Guard, September 10, 2003. www.coloradoguard.com/webpages/dma/familyfocus.htm#_TOC50971888.

Paul Eng, "Making Way for the Hybrids," ABC News, October 1, 2003. abcnews.go.com/sections/SciTech/Business/hybridcars031001-1.html.

Patricia Erickson, "Honoring Military Families," Family First, 2004. www.familyfirst.net/pressroom/veteransday2000.asp.

Dean Esmay, "Discuss This Article," Dean's World, September 29, 2003. www.deanesmay.com/archives/005003.html.

ESPN, "Series Between Seattle, Oakland Canceled," March 18, 2003. http://msn.espn.go.com/mlb/news/2003/0318/1525822.html.

Federal Reserve Board, "Testimony of Chairman Alan Greenspan," February 25, 2004. www.federalreserve.gov/boarddocs/testimony/2004/20040225/default.htm.

Brian J. Foley, "Why the Outrage About Abu Ghraib?" *Counterpunch,* May 15–16, 2004. www.counterpunch.org/foley05152004.html.

C. Benjamin Ford, "Duty, Business Mix for Employers," *Business Gazette,* April 30, 2004. www.gazette.net/200418/business/news/2148171.html.

Fox News, "Iraqi Americans Celebrate Saddam's Capture," December 14, 2003. www.foxnews.com/story/0,2933,105712,00.html.

Joe Garner, "Suicide Sparks Questions," *Rocky Mountain News,* March 18, 2004. www.rockymountainnews.com/drmn/state/article/0,1299,DRMN_21_2738761,00.html.

Bill Gertz, "Turkey Warns It Might Annex Northern Iraq," *World Net Daily,* August 28, 2002. www.worldnetdaily.com/news/printer-friendly.asp?ARTICLE_ID=28760.

Mark Gongloff, "Housing to the Rescue, Again," CNN Money, January 22, 2003. http://money.cnn.com/2003/01/21/news/economy/housing/index.htm.

Ellen Goodman, "The Ugly Americans," *Washington Post,* May 4, 2003. www.postwritersgroup.com/archives/good0503.htm.

James Graff, "The French Resistance," *Time,* February 24, 2003. www.time.com/time/europe/magazine/2003/0224/cover/story_2.html.

Hannity & Colmes, "More Americans: Iraq Worth Going to War," December 15, 2003. http://www.foxnews.com/story/0,2933,105813.00.html.

John Hawkins, "What About the Weapons of Mass Destruction?" *Right Wing News,* 2004. www.rightwingnews.com/john/wmd.php.

John Hendren, "Saddam: A Man with Nothing to Lose," *Sydney Morning Herald,* July 8, 2002. www.smh.com.au/articles/2002/07/07/1025667088589.html.

Kwame Holman, "Background: Talk of War," *Online Newshour,* October 7, 2002. www.pbs.org/newshour/bb/middle_east/july-dec02/bkgdiraqpolls-10-07-02.html.

———, "Iraq Challenge," *Online Newshour,* September 9, 2003. www.pbs.org/newshour/bb/middle_east/july-dec03/iraq_09-09.html.

Mike Hudson, "Economy to Rule Auto Labor Talks," *Detroit News,* July 14, 2003. www.detnews.com/2003/specialreport/0309/08/a01-216641.htm.

John Hughes, "Why Iraq Is Not like Vietnam," *Christian Science Monitor,* August

27, 2003. www.csmonitor.com/2003/0827/ p09s02-cojh.html.

Molly Ivins, "The $87 Billion Question," *Texas Observer,* September 26, 2003. www .texasobserver.org/showArticle.asp? ArticleID=1464.

Al Jazeera, "Soldiers' Families Accuse US of Betrayal," October 2, 2003. http://english .aljazeera.net/NR/exeres/9D65692E-7033-41E2-B8E8-E3B4685C21EA.htm.

Robert Jensen, "Embedded Reporters Viewpoint Misses Main Point of War," Znet, June 8, 2003. www.zmag.org/sustainers/ content/2003-06/08jensen.cfm.

Jeff Johnson, "Democrats Say Establishment Media's Iraq Reporting Biased," Cybercast News Service, September 24, 2003. www.cn snews.com/ViewPentagon.asp?Page=/ Pentagon/archive/200309/PEN2003 0924a.html.

Chris Jolma, "Protest Warriors New Movement," *Washington Times,* November 18, 2003. www.washtimes.com/culture/2003 1117-092208-4242r.htm.

Bart Jones, "Long Island Families Coping with Reservist Delays," Colorado Army National Guard, September 9, 2003, www .coloradoguard.com/webpages/dma/ familyfocus.htm#_TOC50971902.

Eileen Kelley, "Extensions of Duty in Iraq Stir Anger," Colorado Army National Guard, September 10, 2003. www.colorado guard.com/webpages/dma/familyfocus. htm#_Extensions_of_duty.

Louise Kennedy, "Demonstrators Say Peace Movement Will Continue," *Globe,* April 10, 2003. www.mfso.org/Globe1.html.

Robert O. Keohane, "Avoiding the Worst in Iraq," *Raleigh News & Observer,* April 11, 2004. http://newsobserver.com/editorials/ story/3504218p-3108870c.html.

W.F. Keough, "Extended Iraq Tour for Reservists Hits Home Front Hard," Colorado Army National Guard, September 10, 2003. www.coloradoguard.com/webpages/ dma/familyfocus.htm#_TOC50971885.

Jon Krawczynski, "Alabama Hit Hard by Tour Extensions in Iraq," Colorado Army National Guard, September 9, 2003. www .coloradoguard.com/webpages/dma/ familyfocus.htm#_Alabama_hit_hard.

Alan P. Larson, "Future of Iraq," U.S. Department of State, June 4, 2003. www.state .gov/e/rls/rm/2003/21267.htm.

Ryan Lenz, "Soldiers in Iraq Buy Their Own Body Armor," *Guardian Unlimited,* March 26, 2004. www.guardian.co.uk/ worldlatest/story/0,1280,-3904926,00. html.

Joseph Lieberman, "Winning the Wider War Against Terrorism," New Democrats Online, January 14, 2002. www.ndol.org/ ndol_ci.cfm?contentid=250015&kaid=106 &subid=122.

Local 10.com, "Media/Journalism and the War Coverage," March 25, 2003. www .local10.com/news/2062681/detail.html.

Eils Lotozo, "Patriot Act Prompts Outcry by Librarians," Congressman Bernie Saunders Web site, April 19, 2003. http:// bernie.house.gov/documents/articles/ 20030421102754.asp.

Melanie Markley, "Deployment: Family Watches Soldier Go to War—Again," *Houston Chronicle,* March 26, 2003. www

.chron.com/cs/CDA/ssistory.mpl/special/iraq/1836455.

Merissa Marr, "'Embeds' Offer Graphic but Limited War Close-ups," Reuters, March 25, 2003. http://uktop100.reuters.com/latest/Army/top10/20030325-IRAQ-TELEVISION.ASP.

———, "Grisly Images Stoke Media Debate," News 24.com, March 24, 2003. www.news24.com/News24/World/Iraq0,,2-10-1460_1337716,00.html.

Michael Martinez, "Army's Suicide Rate Has Outside Experts Alarmed," Common Dreams News Center, December 30, 2003. www.commondreams.org/headlines03/1230-01.htm.

Maxwell McCombs, "The Agenda-Setting Role of the Mass Media in the Shaping of Public Opinion," Suntory and Toyota International Centres for Economics and Related Disciplines, London School of Economics, 1997. http://sticerd.lse.ac.uk/dps/extra/McCombs.pdf.

Bill Mears, "Supreme Court Looks at 'Enemy Combatants,'" CNN, April 28, 2004. www.cnn.com/2004/LAW/04/27/detainees.

Media Research Center, "In Their Own Words: What Members of the Media Say About Liberal Bias," May 12, 1996. www.mediaresearch.org/biasbasics/welcome.asp#Admissions.

Josh Meyer, "Justice Department Begins New Anti-Terrorist Measures," The Tech, October 26, 2001. www-tech.mit.edu/V121/N54/justice_54.54w.html.

MidEastNews, "Text of British Draft Resolution Presented to Security Council," February 24, 2003. www.mideastnews.com/UKdraft240203.html.

Military Families Speak Out, "Do Not Say That You Are Proud of Me," 2003. www.mfso.org/.

Lorraine Mirabella and Bill Atkinson, "Rising Oil Prices Threaten Economy, Experts Warn," *Baltimore Sun,* May 7, 2004. www.baltimoresun.com/business/bal-te.bz.oil07may07,0,5533727.story?coll=bal-home-headlines.

Dave Moniz, "Some Veterans of Vietnam See Iraq Parallel," *USA Today,* November 7, 2003. www.usatoday.com/news/world/iraq/2003-11-06-vets-usat_x.htm.

Michelle Morgante, "Families of Troops Head to Baghdad on Peace Mission," *Peace Center News,* December 1, 2003. http://peacecalendar.org/archives/2003_12.html.

Dennis Mountjoy, "Iraqi Freedom: A Gift from God," California State Assembly, April 14, 2003. http://republican.assembly.ca.gov/members/index.asp?Dis=59&Lang=1&Body=Opinion Editorials&RefID=535.

Joel Mowbray, "Iraq: Becoming an Islamic Republic?" Townhall.com, October 17, 2003. www.townhall.com/columnists/joelmowbray/printjm20031017.shtml.

Martin J. Moylan, "Cutbacks a Headache for Flyers," Twin Cities.com, May 23, 2003. www.twincities.com/mld/pioneerpress/business/5924482.htm.

MSNBC, "Home Front: One Family's Struggle to Make Ends Meet," 2003. www.msnbc.com/local/KGET/M285909.asp.

Nation, "Antiwar America," March 12, 2003. www.thenation.com/doc.mhtml?i=2003 0331&s=antiwar.

New Democrats Online, "No Divisions in the War on Terror," March 22, 2004. www.ndol.org/ndol_ci.cfm?kaid=131&subid=192&contentid=252467.

News Net 5.com, "Son Killed in Iraq 24 Hours After Talking to Ohio Family," April 12, 2004. www.newsnet5.com/news/2995054/detail.html.

Timothy A. Noah, "Dissent Equals Treason," *Slate,* February 11, 2003. http://slate.msn.com/id/2078455.

NPR, "Citizen Student: Teaching Patriotism in Time of War," February 7, 2003. www.npr.org/display_pages/features/feature_957688.html.

Miles O'Brien, "General Wesley Clark Analyzes Weapons Hunt in Iraq," *CNN Saturday Morning News,* January 18, 2003. www.cnn.com/TRANSCRIPTS/0301/18/smn.05.html.

Online Newshour, "Liberty vs. Security," September 10, 2002. www.pbs.org/newshour/bb/terrorism/july-dec02/liberty_9-10.html.

———, "UN Members Offer Mixed Response to Powell Report," February 5, 2003. www.pbs.org/newshour/updates/reac_02-05-03.html.

Bill O'Reilly, "Media Must Stand Firm Against the Race Card," *New York Daily News,* March 3, 2003. www.nydailynews.com/news/ideas_opinion/story/63940p-59598c.html.

People For the American Way, "Talking Out of Turn: The Right's Campaign Against Dissent," April 29, 2003. www.pfaw.org/pfaw/general/default.aspx?oid=10389.

PhillyBurbs.com, "House Passes Package of Bills to Aid Reservists, Emergency Crews," March 23, 2004. www.phillyburbs.com/pb-dyn/news/103-03232004-269875.html.

Steven Plaut, "Best Examples of Media Bias for the Year, If It Won't Ruin Your Holiday," ChronWatch, January 10, 2004. www.chronwatch.com/content/contentDisplay.asp?aid=5425&catcode=10.

Colin Powell, "Remarks to the United Nations Security Council," U.S. Department of State, February 5, 2003. www.state.gov/secretary/rm/2003/17300.htm.

Prime Minister of Australia Web site, "Transcript of the Prime Minister, the Hon John Howard MP, Address to the Nation," March 20, 2003. www.pm.gov.au/news/speeches/speech79.html.

Kate Randall, "US Army Extends Tours of Guard and Reserve Troops," World Socialist Web Site, September 11, 2003. www.wsws.org/articles/2003/sep2003/arm-s11.shtml.

Chip Reid, "Recalling Life as an Embedded Reporter," MSNBC, March 15, 2004. http://msnbc.msn.com/id/4400708.

Thomas E. Ricks, "Four-Star Marine General: Iraq Strategy 'Screwed-Up,'" Truthout, December 23, 2003. www.truthout.org/docs_03/122403B.shtml.

Matthew Rothschild, "Bush's War Economy," *Progressive,* December 2003. www.progressive.org/dec03/com1203.html.

Rush Online, "Boycott France," March 31, 2003. www.rushonline.com/visitors/france.htm.

Ted Sampley, "US Veteran Dispatch," Vietnam Veterans Against John Kerry, 2004. www.usvetdsp.com/jf_kerry.htm.

Matt Scott, "Unemployment Up: Job Fairs Help Those Looking for Work," WTNH.com March 7, 2003. www.wtnh.com/Global/story.asp?S=1169165.

Ciro Scotti, "Bush's Unfinished Business in Baghdad," *Business Week Online,* January 11, 2002. www.businessweek.com/bwdaily/dnflash/jan2002/nf20020111_3437.htm.

Isaac Shapiro, "Bush Tax Cuts to Send Revenues, as a Share of GDP, to Lowest Level Since 1959," Center on Budget and Policy Priorities, June 4, 2003. www.cbpp.org/6-4-03tax.htm.

David M. Shribman, "Bush Doctrine Slipping Under Political Radar," *Boston Globe,* December 24, 2002. www.kingchuck.com/Iraq/Bush.doctrine1.html.

Robert D. Springer, "Women in Combat," WRAL.com, 2004. www.wral.com/fayettevillenews/890764/detail.html.

Jim Stingl, "A Private Battle," *Milwaukee Journal Sentinel,* October 2, 2003. www.jsonline.com/news/metro/oct03/174439.asp.

St. Petersburg Times, "6 in 10 Oppose Wartime Tax Cuts," April 14, 2003. www.sptimes.com/2003/04/14/Worldandnation/6_in_10_oppose_wartime.shtml

Mike Sunnucks, "McCain Opposes Tax Cuts," *Business Journal,* March 18, 2003. http://phoenix.bizjournal.com/phoenix/stories/2003/03/17/daily29.html.

Tracie L. Takatani, "MCC Students Speak Out," *Ho'oulu Online,* October 10, 2001. http://hooulu.org/10102001/speakout.html.

10 Downing Street, "Part 2: History of Weapons Inspections," May 19, 2004. www.number-10.gov.uk/output/Page277.asp.

Time, "Overview: The US Response," October 10, 2001. www.time.com/time/nation/article/0,8599,178464,00.html.

Ellen Turkenich, "Who Owns the Story: America's Televised Battle for Cultural Supremacy," *Online Journal of Education, Media, and Health,* New York University, 2003. www.nyu.edu/classes/keefer/joe/turkenich.html.

USA Today, "POW Pictures Spark Internet Censorship Debate," Match 26, 2003. www.usatoday.com/tech/world/iraq/2003-03-26-net-censorship_x.htm.

U.S. Department of State, "Rumsfeld Praises Operation Iraqi Freedom Troops," March 20, 2003. http://usinfo.state.gov/topical/pol/terror/03032012.htm.

———, "Violent Minorities Will Not Thwart Iraq's Future, Bremer Says," April 18, 2004. http://usinfo.state.gov/mena/Archive/2004/Apr/18-871777.html.

Tracy Vedder, "New Technology to Defeat Terrorism in Our Ports," KOMO 4 News, March 15, 2004. www.komo1000news.com/news/story.asp?ID=30310.

Rich Vosepka, "More Loneliness Ahead for Utah Guardsmen's Families," Colorado Army National Guard, September 9, 2003. www.coloradoguard.com/webpages/dma/familyfocus.htm#_TOC50971900.

Chuck Wagner, "Study: Network Coverage Fair on Iraq War," *Pentagram,* September 26, 2003. www.dcmilitary.com/army/pentagram/8_38/national_news/25465-1.html.

Kelly Wallace, "James Baker: Don't Go It Alone with Iraq," CNN, August 26, 2002. www.cnn.com/2002/ALLPOLITICS/08/25/iraq.baker/index.html.

Wayne Washington, "Bush Aides Admit Iraq Missteps," *Boston Globe,* September 9, 2003. www.boston.com/news/nation/washington/articles/2003/09/09/bush_aides_admit_iraq_missteps.

The White House, "President Bush Outlines Iraqi Threat," October 7, 2002. www.whitehouse.gov/news/releases/2002/10/20021007-8.html.

———, "President Delivers State of the Union Address," January 29, 2002. www.whitehouse.gov/news/releases/2002/01/20020129-11.html.

———, "The President Says Saddam Hussein Must Leave Iraq Within 48 Hours," March 17, 2003. www.whitehouse.gov/news/releases/2003/03/20030317-7.html.

———, "President's Remarks at the United Nations General Assembly," September 12, 2002. www.whitehouse.gov/news/releases/2002/09/20020912-1.html.

———, "Remarks by Samuel R. Berger, Assistant to the President for National Security Affairs," February 13, 1998. http://clinton4.nara.gov/WH/EOP/NSC/html/speeches/19980213.html.

Gleaves Whitney, "Democrats for Preemption," *National Review Online,* February 13, 2003. www.nationalreview.com/comment/comment-whitney021303.asp.

Marian Wilkinson, "Top US General Raises Spectre of Civil War," *Sydney Morning Herald,* March 5, 2004. www.smh.com.au/articles/2004/03/04/1078378914916.html?from=storyrhs.

Brian Williams, "Helping Soldiers' Families Cope," MSNBC, February 2, 2004. www.msnbc.msn.com/id/4138080.

"World Held Hostage," November 15, 1998. www.geocities.com/CapitolHill/Congress/5747/WorldHeldHostage.html.

Yahoo! News, "Analysts Warned of Iraq War's High Cost," November 1, 2003. http://asia.news.yahoo.com/031101/ap/d7uhm2sg0.html.

Karl Zinsmeister, "Progress Exceeds Prognostication in Iraq," *Christian Science Monitor,* October 20, 2003. www.christiansciencemonitor.com/2003/1020/p09s01-coop.html.

Aaron Zitner, "Ridge Revises Advice: Buy Duct Tape but Wait for a Signal," *Detroit News,* February 15, 2003. www.detnews.com/2003/politics/0302/16/politics-85682.htm.

Gregg Zoroya, "Soldier's Suicide Shocks PA Town," *USA Today,* October 12, 2003. www.usatoday.com/news/nation/2003-10-12-suicide-inside-usat_x.htm.

Mortimer Zuckerman, "The Case for Burden Bearing," Congressman Mark Kennedy Web Site, November 3, 2003. http://markkennedy.house.gov/cgi-data/reading/files/7.shtml.

✫ Index ✫

ABC, 42, 70
Abdul-Aziz, Rana, 83
Abizaid, John, 98
Abu Ghraib prison, 83
Afghanistan, 15, 16, 17, 56, 70, 94
Age, The (Web site), 96
Air Force Aid Society, 59
airline industry, 69–71, 75
airport security, 32, 33, 35
Allied Pilots Association, 75
Alterman, Eric, 89
American Airlines, 75
American Civil Liberties Union, 39
Ames, Joseph, 78
Anderson, Beth, 63
Anderson, Ryan, 30
Annan, Kofi, 91, 92
anthrax, 31
antiwar demonstrations, 81–82
    counterdemonstrators and, 83–85
    media coverage of, 42
Australia, 23
axis of evil, 16–17
Aznar, José Maria, 27

Baath Party, 11
Babbel, Gene, 61
Baghdad (Iraq), 10, 11, 28, 40–41,
    76–77, 95
Baker, James, 22
Bali (Indonesia), 17
Bangladesh, 74
Barr, William, 38
Belgium, 17, 23

Bender, Bryan, 96
Berg, Nicholas, 47
Berger, Nina, 53
Berger, Samuel R., 17–18
Bierwagen, Sandra, 67
bin Laden, Osama, 15, 17
Bitoff, John, 50–51
Black & Decker, 70
Blair, Tony, 27
border security, 32, 35
Boston Globe (newspaper), 19
botulinum bacteria, 28
Bowers, Ted, 64
Brahimi, Lakhdar, 93
Bremer, L. Paul, 95–96
Buchanan, Pat, 88
Buchheit, Peter, 70
Buck, Chuck, 74
Buck Knives, 74
budget deficit, 77–79
Budke, Don, 60
Bureau of Alcohol, Tobacco, Firearms
    and Explosives, 32
Bush, George H.W., 20–21, 29
Bush, George W., 13, 19, 31, 77, 90, 94
    administration of, 25, 76, 78, 83, 85, 86,
        88, 90
    controversy over, 89
    declining popularity of, 46
    personal motive of, for war, 20–21
    rationale of, for war, 9–10
    State of the Union addresses of, 16–17,
        26–27
    ultimatums issued by, 18, 27

victory claimed by, 11
war on terror supported by, 15–17
Byrd, Robert C., 86
Byrne, Gloria, 57

Canada, 23, 32
CBS, 42
Cenotti, Angelo, 74
Center for Media and Public Affairs, 42
Center for Strategic and International
  Studies, 28
Central Intelligence Agency (CIA), 32,
  96
CertifiChecks, 59
Chalabi, Ahmad, 87, 88
Chen, David, 40–41
Cheney, Dick, 86
China, 17, 74
Chirac, Jacques, 23
Christian Science Monitor (Web site), 47
citizen soldiers, 57
civil liberties, 36–39
Civil War, 38
Clark, Gordon, 83
Clark, Wesley, 20, 90
Clarke, Richard, 29
Clinton, Bill, 17
Clinton, Hillary, 87
CNN, 41–42, 47, 48
coalition of the willing, 23
Coalition Provisional Authority, U.S., 95
Coast Guard, U.S., 32
Computer Assisted Passenger
  Prescreening System II (CAPPS II),
  38–39
*Connecticut Yankee in King Arthur's Court,
  A* (Twain), 84
Corbett, Brian, 58
Corrigan, Katie, 39
Cowling, Jamie, 52
Cuban Missile Crisis, 20

Daniels, Mitchell, 35–36
Daschle, Tom, 84
Defense Department, U.S., 49–51
Dellevigne, Paul, 21
Democratic Party, 85, 87, 93
Dent, Darryl T., 63
Diamonde, Judy, 12
Dickerson, John F., 89
Dickey, Christopher, 28–29
DiCola, Connie, 55
Dietz, Richard, 21
dirty bombs, 34, 37
Donnelly, Sally B., 34
Dow Jones Industrial Average, 68–69
Drug Enforcement Administration, 32
Dunn, Daniel, 11

Eastern Airlines, 71
economy
  deficit return and, 77–79
  rebound of, 79–80
  rebuilding of Iraq and, 75–77, 78
  slump in, 68–70
  wait-and-see attitude toward, 70–71
embedding, 51–53
enemy combatants, 29, 36–37
Erickson, Patricia, 54
European Union, 24

Faris, Iyman, 30
Federal Bureau of Investigation (FBI),
  29, 32, 36, 37, 39
Federal Emergency Management
  Agency, 32, 48
Felling, Matthew, 42
female combatants, 64–65
Fischer, Joschka, 26
Fish, Mike, 48
Fisher House, 59–60
Flynn, Phil, 73
Foley, Brian J., 83

Fonda, Daren, 34
Fought, Stephanie, 65, 66
Fox, Beverly, 65
Fox News, 41–42, 48
France, 22–25, 26
Franks, Tommy, 90
Freedom fries, 24
Frist, Bill, 33

Gallup polls, 40, 42
Garner, Jay, 89
General Motors, 75
Geneva Convention, 36–37, 47
Germany, 17, 19, 22–23, 26, 77
Gertz, Bill, 96–97
Gibbs, Nancy, 14
Gingrich, Newt, 90
Goldstein, Thomas, 37
Gongloff, Mark, 70
Gonsales, Denise, 55, 56
Goodman, Ellen, 83
Good Morning America (TV series), 48
Great Britain, 23
Greenspan, Alan, 79–80
Guerra, Frank, 58
Guerra, Lilly, 58
Gunaratna, Rohan, 95
Gundersen, Diana, 54–55

Haas, Richard, 15
habeas corpus, 38
Haiti, 36
Halabja (Iraq), 20
Hannity, Sean, 42
Harkness, Stephanie, 70
Harris, Jacki, 78
Hawkins, John, 88
Heatwole, Nathaniel, 33, 34
Henry, Earl, 75
Heritage (magazine), 24
Homeland Security Office, 31–32, 49

housing market, 70, 79
Howard, John, 23
Hughes, John, 47
Hussein, Saddam, 10, 15, 23, 25, 28, 36,
    77, 84, 85–87, 89, 94, 95, 99
  assassination attempt of, on Bush Sr.,
    21, 29
  capture of, 9, 11, 12, 79, 81
  debate on threat posed by, 20–22
  oil supplies and, 71, 72
  statues of, toppled, 44
  support for overthrow of, 88
  ultimatums issued to, 18, 27
  UN inspections thwarted by, 17–18, 26
hybrid cars, 73

India, 74
Indonesia, 74
Institute of Public Policy Research, 52
interest rates, 70, 79
Internet, 47
Iran, 16, 17, 71
Iran-Iraq War, 20
Iraqi Americans, 36
Iraq Pledge of Resistance, 83
al-Islam, Ansar, 26
Isom, Michelle, 61
Israel, 25
Ivins, Molly, 77

James, Mary, 69–70
Japan, 19, 23, 77
Al Jazeera (media station), 43
Jenson, Robert, 43
job market, 74–75
Johnson, Claude, 64–65
Johnson, Lyndon, 46
Johnson, Shoshana, 45, 53, 64–65

Kadlec, Daniel, 78
Kay, David, 87

Kennedy, Edward, 19, 76
Kennedy, John F., 20
Keohane, Robert O., 80
Kerry, John, 93–94
Khatami, Mohammed, 17
Klaidman, Daniel, 28–29
Klein, Joe, 94
Kuesel, Robert, 12
Kurds, 88, 89, 96–97
Kuwait, 71, 94

LaRocque, Ed, 73
Larson, Alan P., 99
Leber, Matt, 81
Liberty toast, 24
librarians, PATRIOT Act and, 37–38
Libya, 71
Lieberman, Joe, 98
Lincoln, Abraham, 38
Lindauer, Susan, 30
Lindenberg, Ashlee, 57
Liu, Melinda, 10
Lopercio, Michael, 12
Los Angeles Times (newspaper), 48
Lott, Trent, 87
Lynch, Jessica, 44–46

MacLeod, Meagan, 9
Maddox, Tony, 47
Mahdi Army, 96
Mark, Jason, 82
al-Marri, Ali, 29
Marshall, Jim, 44
McCain, John, 79
McCombs, Maxwell, 39
McInerney, Tom, 46
media, 12, 39
  access of, to the war, 49–53
  bias in, 40–43
  drama emphasized by, 43–46
  fear promoted by, 47–49

Middle Eastern, 43
  speculation by, 46
Meis, Dick, 12
Mexico, 32
Meyer, Josh, 38
military families
  assistance for, 59–60
  casualties and, 61–63
  courage of, 55–57
  economic hardship in, 58–59
  homecomings and, 65–67
  sacrifices made by, 54–55
Military Families Speak Out (Web site),
  61
Motorola Communications Electronics,
  59
Mountjoy, Dennis, 12
Murdoch, Rupert K., 41
Murray, Patty, 34
Al-Musaib (Iraq), 40
Muslims, 27, 85, 88, 89, 96, 97
Mylott, Jennifer, 56

An-Nasiriya (Iraq), 40
Nassiriya (Iraq), 44
Nation (magazine), 86
National Bio-Weapons Defense Analysis
  Center, 32
National Communications System, 32
National Guard, 57, 58, 61, 63
National Gulf War Resource Center, 64
Nazi Germany, 19
NBC, 42, 51
Negroponte, John, 16
Newsweek (magazine), 10, 12, 42, 56
New York Sun (newspaper), 84
New York Times (newspaper), 40
Niederer, Sue, 81
Nike, 74
no-fly zones over Iraq, 18, 86, 88
North Korea, 16, 17

Norway, 23
nuclear weapons, 17, 20

Offutt, Jean, 45
oil, 71–73, 79
Omar, Mohammed, 17
101st Airborne Division, 48
129th Transportation Company, 60
Operation Iraqi Freedom, 90
O'Reilly, Bill, 40
Organization of the Petroleum
  Exporting Countries (OPEC), 73
Orszag, Peter, 79

Padilla, José, 37
Pakistan, 17
Palestine, 25
Pan Am, 71
Paris Air Show (2003), 24–25
Pentagon, 24–25, 32, 60
Perle, Richard, 24
Persian Gulf War, 20–21, 27, 50, 71, 86, 88
Pethokoukis, James M., 71
Philbrick, Walter, 31
Plass, Michael, 59
polls, 15, 22, 40, 42
Poniewozik, James, 43
port security, 34
Powell, Colin, 25–26, 27, 87
power failures, 32–33
preemptive war
  American reactions to, 18–20
  international reactions to, 22–23
presidential campaign (2004), 12–13,
  93–94
prisoners of war (POWs), 36–37
  female, 64–65
  media coverage of, 44–46
Prius (car), 73

al Qaeda, 15, 17, 23, 37, 68, 85

Saddam linked to, 25–26
  in the U.S., 29–30
Qatar, 71

rebuilding of Iraq, 89
  cost of, 75–77, 78
  UN and, 90–93
Reid, Chip, 51, 53
Reliance Armor, 60
Republican Party, 86–87
reservists, 57–59, 60, 61, 63
retail sales, 70
Rice, Condoleezza, 46, 86
ricin, 33
Ridge, Tom, 31, 32, 35, 49
Rivera, Geraldo, 48
Robertson, Pat, 84
Robinson, Steve, 64
Rodriguez, Paula, 57–58
Rostan, Sandi, 65
Rothschild, Matthew, 74
Rubin, Robert, 79
Rumsfeld, Donald, 15, 46, 86
Russia, 22–23, 26

al-Samoud missiles, 23
sarin, 20
Saudi Arabia, 71
Schermerhorn, Sky, 12
Scotti, Ciro, 20–21
Scowcroft, Brent, 85, 86
Scud missiles, 28
Second Battalion, 12
Secret Service, U.S., 32
security measures, 28–39
  alarming accidents and, 32–33
  concerns about civil liberties and,
    36–39
  increased government power and,
    36–38
  limitations of, 34–36

personal, 30–31
Selig, Bud, 30
September 11 terrorist attacks, 15, 17, 28, 31, 36, 94
  Baghdad attacks compared with, 41
  economic impact of, 68–70, 77
Shaikh Mohammed, Khalid, 29–30
Shapiro, Isaac, 78
Shelkrot, Elliot, 37–38
Sherman, Lawrence, 32
Shiite Muslims, 88, 89, 96
Shribman, David M., 19
Sinai, Allan, 79
Small, Corcy, 63–64
smallpox virus, 28–29
Smart, Elizabeth, 53
Smith, Sam, 60
Snowe, Olympia, 79
Somalia, 50
South Korea, 17
Soviet Union, 19, 20
Spain, 17, 23, 27
Spratt, John, 56
Springer, Robert D., 65
State Department, U.S., 15, 32
State of the Union addresses, 16–17, 26–27
stock market, 68–69, 79
Sudan, 17
Suell, Joseph, 64
Suell, Rebecca, 64
suicide, of military personnel, 63–64
Sullivan, Andrew, 22
Sunni Muslims, 89, 96
Supreme Court, U.S., 37
Swonk, Diane, 68
Sydney Morning Herald (Web site), 98

Taliban, 15, 17
tax cuts, 78–79
Taylor, Curtis, 29

Taylor, William, 28
Tech, The (Web site), 38
terrorism, 11, 12
  Saddam linked with, 25–26
  war against, 15–17
  watch lists for, 39
  see also security measures; September 11 terrorist attacks
Terrorist Screening Center, 39
Terrorist Threat Integration Center, 39
Thomas, Evan, 42
Thorne-Henderson, Margaret, 53
Time (magazine), 15, 29, 34, 43, 72, 77, 89
Toyota North America, 73
Tracey, James, 43
Tragedy Assistance Program for Survivors (TAPS), 62
Tramco Mold, Inc., 58
Tumulty, Karen, 89
Tunisia, 17
Turkenich, Ellen, 45
Turkey, 96
Turner, Ted, 41
Twain, Mark, 84

Umm Qasr (Iraq), 40
unemployment rate, 74, 79
unions, 75
United Arab Emirates, 73
United Auto Workers, 75
United Nations (UN), 88, 94
  Afghanistan occupation and, 17
  reaction of, to proposed war, 16, 22, 23, 25
  rebuilding of Iraq and, 90–93
  Resolution 1441, 26, 27
  Security Council, 16, 25, 27
  weapons inspections by, 9, 17–18, 26, 86, 87
United Service Organizations (USO), 59

USA PATRIOT Act, 37–39
USA Today (Web site), 51
U.S. News & World Report (magazine), 14, 71

vaccines, 30, 31
Valentini, Penny, 58
Valentini, Ted, 58
Vandayburg, Allen, 62
Veale, Jennifer, 67
Vieira de Mello, Sergio, 92
Vietnam Veterans Against the War, 94
Vietnam War, 46, 47, 50, 82, 83, 93, 94
Villepin, Dominique de, 26
Vining, Cindy, 67

Wal-Mart, 74
Walt Disney Company, 70
Wamp, Zack, 77
weapons of mass destruction (WMDs), 86

alleged evidence of, 25–26
failure to find, 81
inspections for, 9, 17–18, 26, 86, 87
missing, 87–88
speculation about, 15, 17, 20, 28, 29
Wendelstedt, Hunter, 71
White, Mary Jo, 36
Wilhelm, Pete, 81
Wilkinson, Marian, 98
Wolfowitz, Paul, 91
World Socialist (Web site), 63
World War II, 23, 77
Wray, Ann, 56

Zagorin, Adam, 72
Zangana, Alan, 9
Zinn, Howard, 84–85
Zinni, Anthony, 46, 85–86
Zoberg, Alexis, 83
Zuckerman, Mortimer, 90

★ Picture Credits ★

✯ About the Author ✯

Diane Yancey works as a freelance writer in the Pacific Northwest, where she has lived for twenty-five years. She writes nonfiction for middle-grade and high school readers and enjoys traveling and collecting old books. Some of her other books are *Life in War-Torn Bosnia, Leaders and Generals (War on Terrorism),* and *Life of an American Soldier in Afghanistan.*